Agile Software Development with Distributed Teams

Staying Agile in a Global World

Jutta Eckstein

Agile Software Development with Distributed Teams

Staying Agile in a Global World

Jutta Eckstein

ISBN 978-3-947991-27-3

Cover design and chapter illustrations: Katja Gloggengießer, www.grellgelb.de URL of the book for updates etc.: https://www.jeckstein.com/agile-in-the-large/ No part of this book may be reproduced or transmitted in any form or by any means, electronic or mechanical, including photocopying, recording, or by any information storage and retrieval system, without written permission from the author. Every precaution was taken in the preparation of this book. However, the author and publisher assume no responsibility for errors or omissions, or for damages that may result from the use of the information contained in this book.

Contents

CONTENTS

Acknowledgments

Books are in the air.
The author provides only a bridge between material and tran-
script.

– Marguerite Duras

One significant problem with conducting such a project as writing a book is remembering all the people who have supported me. This is, in my opinion, a problem that is unsolvable because almost everyone with whom I communicated during—and even before starting—this project has contributed by sharing experiences or providing feedback.

Unfortunately, it is impossible for me to remember everyone I've met with in the past ten years. Therefore, I begin my acknowledgments by apologizing in advance to those I fail to mention explicitly. They are the people on teams all over the world with whom I have had the opportunity to work while learning not only about agile software development, but also similarities and differences between cultures, interactions, and, not least of all, food, food, glorious food. These contributors are as well the countless people who have helped me reflect on my experiences, enabling me to transform and codify what I learned into something tangible and explicit. I am grateful for time spent with these reflection partners, whom I've met at workshops, talks, tutorials, and panels at many different conferences—the conference of the Association of C and C++ Users, ACCU in the United Kingdom, Agile in North America, Java And Object-Oriented, JAOO in Denmark, Retrospective Gathering in North America and Europe, and XP in Europe, to name just a few.

To those whose names gratitude has made indelible in my memory, I also give thanks: David Hussman, Naresh Jain, Nicolai Josuttis, Daniel Karlström, Michael Kircher, Debra Lavell, Ainsley Nies, Joseph Pelrine, and Linda Rising, I am ever indebted to each of you for writing an expert box for this book, thus sharing your invaluable experience and providing an additional perspective on the subject at hand.

Thanks as well to my reviewers for generously sharing their considerable knowledge and for guiding my attempts to get it right in a book: Jamie Allsop, Joseph Bergin, Magnus Christerson, Lise Hvatum, Carsten Jakobsen, Michael Kircher, Yi Lv, Ken Pugh, Bas Vodde—you are the best.

To Wendy Eakin, Claire Veligdan, and all the folks at Dorset House Publishing, thank you for again proving that editorial standards still fly high. For professionalism in turning my work into a readable book, *Danke schön.*

Last—but definitely not least—I give thanks and more to my family, who never seem to grow bored listening to my stories of travel and work, forever helping me see differences and similarities among people around the world. Foremost, I give thanks to my partner, Nicolai Josuttis, who not only provides great support for my professional life but, even more importantly, enriches my personal life in most wonderful ways; to my cousin Katja Gloggengiesser, whose delightful illustrations make this book more vivid; and finally, to my sister, Eva Eckstein, whose brilliant recommendation again encouraged me to write about global projects while hidden away on Hiddensee, the same little island in the Baltic Sea where I wrote *Agile Software Development in the Large.* I thank you, all!

Preface

We are all called to be pontifeces–bridge builders.
Various rivers have already a crossing.
At many others we are standing at diverse watersides
And we are looking for pontoons,
For a footbridge, for communication.
No sea is separating creation and technology,
But often speechlessness.

– August Everding

Several years back when I was preparing the manuscript for *Agile Software Development in the Large,* I encountered only a few people scaling agile methods up to use on large projects, teams, and organizations. Since then, many people have discovered that agility works for projects of all sizes, that agile methods are not only applicable on small teams.

There is, I have learned, a big difference between the mostly large projects I worked with five years ago and the ones I work with now. To my mind, the most significant difference is that almost all large projects today comprise work and teams spread over multiple locations and time zones. These days, even small projects are not necessarily collocated.

For me, the biggest change between then and now is that I have to travel a lot when serving distributed projects as change agent, project coach, or consultant. I find this exhilarating—and yes, at the same time, exhausting—because travel furnishes me with many amazing opportunities to learn about different processes and cultures. One lesson learned is that my experiences in scaling agile processes up can be transferred to distributed projects, because distributed and large projects hide some of the same issues, but there are a lot of other challenges that are more difficult to overcome and that require special attention if you don't want to lose overall agility when spread over the globe.

Consequently, I've made the focal point of this book the many distributed software development projects that successfully follow an agile approach. My objective is to illuminate best practices for applying agility when project members spread over the globe. I hope you will find the material in this book both helpful and enjoyable to read, possibly even taking the book on one of your trips to one of *your* distributed teams. Whatever the circumstances, I am curious to learn about your experiences and invite you to visit the book's Website[1].

---

[1] http://distributed-teams.com

1. Getting Started

Experience precedes theory.

— Jean-Jacques Rousseau

Today, there are not many large, software-development projects left that are developed "at home" without outsourcing or offshoring. Both outsourcing and offshoring dictate distance between project members. The distance can be geographical, temporal, cultural, linguistical, political, and/or historical. Offshore projects often involve not just one form of distance but, rather, a combination of types of distance. To manage such projects, more and more software-development project architects regard agility as a critical success factor. One reason for this is that agile software development emphasizes face-to-face communication and close collaboration between all project members.

Despite the seeming incompatibility of distributed software development and agile methods, many projects have successfully combined them. Success depends upon colleagues addressing communication constraints and barriers in a distributed setting by emphasizing the importance of communication and interactions among all who contribute to the development. Agile methods promote exactly that.

However, the Agile Manifesto[1] and its underlying principles do not argue against the feasibility of agility in a distributed setting and agile principles can help you to keep the necessary focus in your development approach in order to stay agile and to maximize the potential of the communication mediums at your disposal, no matter how constrained they are. Although when conducting distributed agile software development you might not find a specific agile methodology that can be used out-of-the-box, it is worth your while to explore all options.

For more than a decade, I have worked with large, globally distributed projects. Typically, my projects comprise seventy to

---

[1] To read the Agile Manifesto, see: http://agilemanifesto.org.

three-hundred project team members distributed over three to five locations. Some of the projects involved four locations all within Europe; others spread across South America, Europe, and Asia. The domain of these projects varied greatly: Some were commercial applications; most were technical (for example, embedded systems). The experiences I share in this book come from my work on these large, global, agile projects in embedded and commercial software development. These experiences demonstrate that large—and even distributed—teams can benefit from the same agile value system that benefits small, collocated teams.

My Focus

My first goal in *Agile Software Development with Distributed Teams* is to reconcile two mainstays of modern agility: distributed project teams and close collaboration. The book is about developing software with a single team or with multiple, distributed teams. Distributed development involves facing challenges related to bringing together different teams from different countries, and ensuring that all team members—wherever they're located—work toward the same goals, despite distances between them. The book also describes how to develop solutions to these challenges. It does not address providing a service or an infrastructure from an offshore location and managing it from a home location as it is for example required for running a distant call center.

My Intended Audience

You will find that even if your project is distributed within a single country or even within one town—for example, ten team members working from their home offices or twenty team members distributed over several floors in a building—you can benefit from the material in this book, which is written for people looking for a way to become more flexible and agile although they work in a distributed setting. I include a basic foundation for agile development that I hope will be helpful even if you have already acquired some knowledge of this approach.

For people already familiar with agile development but who have experienced it only in a collocated setting, this book offers guidance on how to apply agility in a distributed setting.

For change agents who want to benefit from both agile and distributed development factors while working on a global team as project managers, process coaches, customer representatives, consultants, or developers, this book should be of particular interest. It is especially relevant to the following:

- People who have tried to use agile methodologies in distributed projects but have failed.
- People who have not tried agile methodologies in distributed projects but would like to do so.
- People who are firm believers of agile processes, but who think they would never work in a distributed setting.

My Perspective

There are many books that can help you decide whether offshoring makes sense for you.[2] This book, however, assumes that the decision to conduct at least part of the project offshore has already been made, taking offshoring as a given. As Sandberg and Skår observe, "Offshoring is here to stay. We have to live with it and try to make the best of it."[3]

For reasons that should become clear as you continue reading, I do not delve into the topic of job insecurity—people's fear of employment exportation—but I do describe how jobs at a base location will change in a distributed project and how people must adjust so as to work effectively across different locations (and shores).

1.1 Roadmap to the Book

In order to plan a beneficial route through this book, please consider the following overview of topics covered, and choose chapters according to your specific interests:

---

[2] If you are looking for in-depth information about offshore projects, I suggest you read M.F. Corbett's *The Outsourcing Revolution: Why It Makes Sense and How to Do It Right*, Thomas L. Friedman's *The World is Flat. A Brief History of the Twenty-First Century*, M.C. Lacity and L.P. Willcocks' *Global Information Technology Outsourcing: In Search of Business Advantage*, and N. Thondavadi and G. Albert's *Offshore Outsourcing: Path to New Efficiencies in IT and Business Processes*.

[3] J.-E. Sandberg and L. A. Skår in a workshop on "Can Agile Practices Deliver High-Quality, Large-Scale Offshored Projects?" at XP 2007 Conference, Como, Italy, 2007.

- Chapter Two, "Assessing Agility and Distributed Projects," lays the foundation for understanding both distributed and agile software development. The chapter explains what makes a project distributed as well as the fundamentals of agile development and then investigates how agile principles influence distributed development.
- Chapter Three, "Building Teams," provides guidance on structuring teams in a distributed agile setting, describes how feature teams will enable a project to consistently deliver the highest business value at any point during the project's lifetime, defines necessary project roles, and ends with information on how team members can maintain conceptual integrity with diverse feature teams in place.
- Chapter Four, "Establishing Communication and Trust," explores how team members and leaders can plan and create trusting relationships between each distributed site, and stresses the importance of building mutual respect among all project members. Based on the idea that trust needs touch, the chapter examines how proximity can be created despite distance by promoting communication among all project locations. It also considers how cultural differences influence communication and trust.
- Chapter Five, "Keeping Sites in Touch," focuses on the roles and responsibilities that are essential to establishing and preserving good working relationships between all sites. It details how to recruit team members to serve as communication facilitators who will travel between all locations as ambassadors representing their home location. It also considers ways to build and strengthen social connections through the use of virtual tools.
- Chapter Six, "Ensuring Development and Delivery," explains agile development cycles in terms of iterations marking short- and long-term releases throughout the project plan. Because agile methods focus on delivery, the chapter provides a discussion of system infrastructure as well as of system integration and build.
- Chapter Seven, "Ensuring Business Value," presents ways to steer the development effort by focusing on features that provide the highest-possible business value at any point in time. The chapter describes how to use a project's velocity—its speed of development—to plan and track not only each iteration but also the overall project plan, and works through methods for coping with change without sacrificing on-time delivery or best-possible business value.

- Chapter Eight, "Eliciting Feedback and Conducting Retrospectives," addresses ways to involve customers in review meetings to elicit feedback on the system, as well as how to conduct retrospectives to continuously improve the development process. The chapter also includes information on what kinds of metrics can be used to measure the progress and quality of the development effort.
- Chapter Nine, "Customizing Practices," emphasizes how to adjust and compose development and process practices that will help teams stay agile while supporting specific needs, and discusses ways to hone and customize practices to help establish and preserve a development culture throughout a project. The chapter also reflects on how elements developed in the Carnegie-Mellon Capability Maturity Model (CMMI) may or may not be useful to you.
- Chapter Ten, "Introducing Agility into New and Existing Distributed Projects," explains how to get started implementing agile development in a distributed setting. If you're starting a new project, the chapter recommends that you advocate agile concepts first locally and then globally, and treats ways to "grow" agile teams and project sites. The book's concluding discussion details how to introduce an agile approach into an existing distributed project, which takes our attention to a new "starting point" but ends treatment of the topics in this book.

At the end of the book are a glossary and references pointing to further readings in recommended articles, books, and URLs.

2. Assessing Agility and Distributed Projects

All things are connected.

— Chief Seattle

2.1 Understanding Distributed Development

My neighborhood grocery store currently displays an advertisement that notes,

> Computer specialists can be found in India; a grocery specialist is just around the corner.

One message to be taken from this ad is that people may need to go far afield to find experts to build or support technology, but they easily can find everything they want in the way of non-technological expertise locally. I don't want to argue for or against the cultural bias of this supposition (there undoubtedly are myriad grocery specialists in India, and I know for certain that there are IT specialists by the thousands in Germany), but I do want to note the implied difference in difficulty between seeking experts locally versus abroad. That's not to imply that the difficulty in looking for talented people in more than one place argues against globalization, merely that global project success involves more than just hiring top performers from around the world. Of course, there are those cynics who say that going global just means that the project will fail cheaper, so if cheap labor is the main goal, then just looking for any kind of cheap help will be enough.

As when shopping for groceries, software customers require at a minimum a local contact from whom to receive the actual product. Globalization does not change this. Although global software development may encompass multiple locations, distributed and dispersed teams, numerous companies, and off-site customers, a "local" coordinator only becomes more important as project scope, distance, and dispersion increase. Simulating proximity is one key to the success of distributed projects, as will be seen in the following sections.

Working With Several Development Sites

As indicated previously, a typical setting in a distributed software development effort involves multiple development sites. Project experts should not all be physically clustered at one site, but instead can communicate their knowledge virtually, across even several countries. In this way, each expert is the local link to the dispersed project effort.

Obvious difficulties accompany the geographical distribution of project experts. Experts must collaborate despite being located at different sites, but different cultures, time zones, languages, distance, and so on, make collaboration difficult. The goal is for experts to communicate with each other, then translate their specific duties to the local audience.

Distributed and Dispersed Teams

At the core of distributed development are teams at multiple sites. A distributed project may be staffed by one or both of the following kinds of teams:

- *Distributed teams* might be made up of one group of people located in, say, Bangalore, India, and another group in the United States. This work unit is *distributed* between two sites, and the project is made up of two teams situated at different sites. Staff may work on different aspects of a project, but they form a single work unit (like an offensive and defensive squad on the same sports team).
- A *dispersed team* is one unit that is made up of people working at numerous locations. One team member may be located in India, another one in Northern Ireland, a third in the United States, and a fourth in Russia, with all four working as one development team.

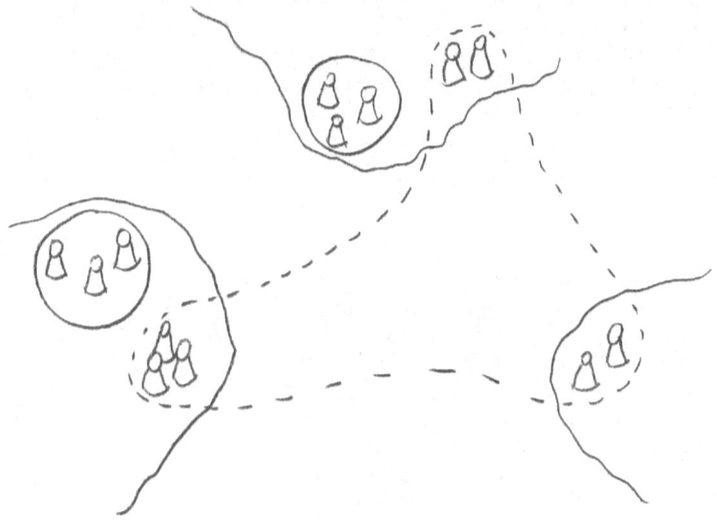

Dispersed Teams

Most often, large global software-development projects include a mix of distributed teams as well as dispersed teams. Some groups within such a project may be collocated while others communicate from outposts. Keep in mind that a dispersed team requires a high coordination effort, even if the team is small, in order to ensure effective communication among all team members. Commit to building team identity early on in order to ensure that all members work toward the same goal.

Large Projects

Developing a project globally usually increases its size. As explored in [Eckstein04], factors that determine a project's size include scope, time, budget, people, and risk. For example, factors other than budget certainly contribute to a project's complexity and stature. The relationship between such factors as people and time also affect the size and nature of projects— few distributed projects are scheduled to last only three months, as it is just not worth the effort to set up a heavily dispersed environment with every team member in a different part of the world. Large projects, whether distributed or not, always garner their own risks. One risk is attendant with the coordination of diverse people and teams. Another is ensuring that a large project remains flexible and efficient, despite the overhead required, for example, to ensure that all project members have the same goals in mind.

Coordinating Companies

Often, the expertise of more than one company can provide better value for software customers than can be provided by a single entity. Some companies deem appropriate the strategy either of buying a company in order to work with teams at different sites or of founding a subsidiary at a different location, thereby ensuring an enduring cooperation and committing long-term to global development. Other companies regard distributed development as a chance to focus on their own core competency, and they prefer, therefore, to outsource peripheral tasks to other companies. Others use distributed development as an opportunity to better recruit talent.

No matter the group's formal organization, the effort to bring together different companies for a project requires a considerable amount of work to establish cordial, and essentially trusting, relationships between parties. A lack of mutual respect may cause difficulty between different subsidiaries, but it spells disaster when between different companies.

The kind of relationship coordinating companies seek can be defined in a contract, which clarifies in detail what two or more parties expect and how they will resolve conflict. By spelling out penalties, contracts provide a formal means to protect involved parties. Although a contract may serve as a means to establish a successful and trusting relationship, it does not actually *create and preserve* a trustworthy relationship that enables successful cooperation. Establishing a complete and successful relationship requires more than just words in a contract. It requires trust and partnership.

The concept of lean development, which is the root of agile development, favors partnerships.[1] Carsten Ruseng Jakobsen,

---

[1] For more information on lean development, see J.K. Liker's *The Toyota Way: 14 Management Principles from the World's Greatest Manufacturer* and Mary and Tom Poppendieck's *Lean Software Development. An Agile Toolkit*. Addison-Wesley, 2003.

Project Manager at the Danish firm Systematic Software Engineering, notes the use and role of contracts in building trusting relationships:

"Toyota has proven that treating sub-contractors as partners instead of continuously seeking [whoever offers] the lowest possible price is more profitable in the long term. . . . Even though you have a contract between different parts of the project, you want the complete project to collaborate toward the same vision."[2]

Different Sites

Distributed projects can encompass any of the following intra- and inter-corporate relationships, each of which engenders unique challenges to the goal of ensuring close collaboration and, thus, success.

- *Offshore outsourcing* occurs when the domestic company outsources all or part of its software development to vendors offshore. Thus, the onshore and offshore companies are different companies, a situation that requires close attention to legal negotiation.[3]
- *Offshore insourcing* occurs when a company founds a subsidiary or buys a separate company located offshore. In such a case, only one company is involved but is itself distributed across the globe. Large multinational organizations, such as General Electric, Schlumberger, International Business Machines, or SAP (spell out??), typically pursue this strategy, primarily to gain market presence offshore.
- *Onshore outsourcing* occurs when one company carries out part of another company's development project. Both companies operate on the same shore, frequently in the same country or at least close by. Onshore outsourcing is not always considered to be global unless it shares many of the challenges of global development, such as

---

[2]C.R. Jakobsen, personal communication.

[3]According to B.B.M. Shao and J Smith-David, despite the logistical difficulties, offshore outsourcing is becoming increasingly popular. See "The Impact of Offshore Outsourcing on IT Workers in Developed Countries: Examining the Global Implications of Outsourcing for IT Workers," *Communications of the ACM*, Vol. 50, No. 2 (February 2007), pp. 89-94.

cultural differences, which may interrupt communication, especially when due to discrepancies between corporate cultures. Perhaps the most significant challenge occurs when programmers, testers, database administrators, and other team members are not collocated.[4]

- *Nearshoring* can be combined with both insourcing as well as outsourcing. The major difference to the preceding settings is while both companies are located on the same shore they are not situated in the same country. For example a Californian based firm sourcing parts of the development activities out to Mexico.

Customers and Distance

Communication *between customers and developers* is similarly important and challenging, as it is *among developers*. Customers must communicate requirements to developers, who, in turn, must fully understand the customers' needs in order to translate them into product functionality. Doing so is difficult even when customers and developers are collocated. It grows more difficult when physical distance and cultural and linguistic differences exist.

When requirements are unclear, developers can gain a better understanding by means of short feedback loops to clarify requirements verbally or to present an early version of the desired product or system. How successful the feedback loops are can depend on the physical distance between customers and developers—particularly when software must work on various platforms and systems, or display in different languages.[5]

Effective, accurate communication among customers and developers plays a major role in a project's success not only during development but also during planning, taking into account different legal requirements and diverse cultural backgrounds.

Centrally Coordinated or Globally Integrated

In his book *Global Software Teams,* Erran Carmel of American University identifies three evolutionary stages of the global

---

[4] Ibid. According to Shao and Smith-David, many outsourcing contracts are based on the strategy of onshore outsourcing.

[5] Thanks to Rachel Davies for pointing this out.

development process. As Carmel sees it, at Stage I, the entire development process takes place at one location, and thus is not a global effort. At Stage II, development takes place at multiple sites, all of which are centrally coordinated and controlled by one headquarters. At Stage III, remote sites are self-directed, with coordination between sites operating like a network. Carmel posits that most software development companies function at Stage II, and only a few companies ever prepare to move to Stage III, in which ". . . various remote development sites assume greater responsibility for a range of tasks and coordinate some activities among themselves without funneling all decisions through headquarters."[6]

Many development efforts even run aground due to company policies that prevent them from advancing to Stage III. These efforts are limited to always assembling the higher management of a product at one location, typically at corporate headquarters.

---

[6]E. Carmel, *Global Software Teams: Collaborating Across Borders and Time Zones* (Englewood Cliffs, N.J.: Prentice Hall, 1999), p. 138.

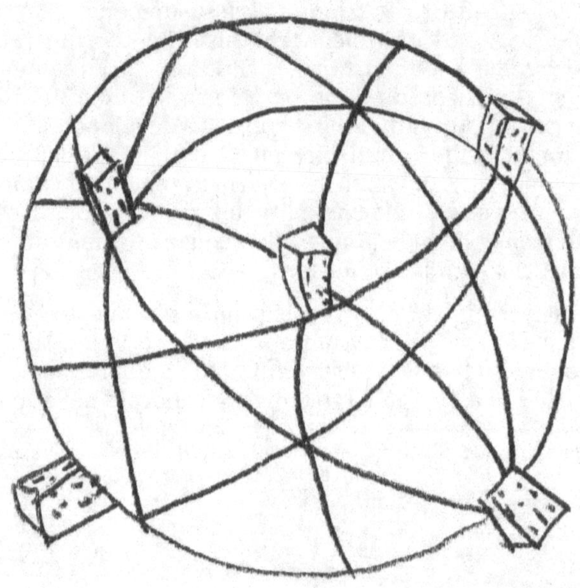

Global Integration

Overcoming the Distance

As now should be evident, distributed development involves much more than just finding (low-cost) experts somewhere. Rather, in order to successfully implement distributed development, the factors discussed above—multiple work sites, large projects, different companies drawn together, and distant customers, must all be addressed. The key to successful distributed development is establishing proximity despite all forms of distance.

2.2 Understanding Agility

A historic marker indicating that agile methods no longer would be considered mere hype or a fringe movement was Scott Adams' *Dilbert* comic strip on agility. With every passing year, agile concepts have become more firmly entrenched in mainstream business and, today, are largely accepted in the modern market. Of course, while noting the movement of agile methods from the realm of fringe, Adams also exposes typical misunderstandings, ill-formed expectations, and downright strange interpretations that some think still pervade the agile approach.[7]

Agility has come into its own as a value system defined by the Agile Manifesto.[8] Based on twelve principles created to ensure the value system,[9] the Agile Manifesto demonstrates that there is more to agile development than just one specific methodology, such as Extreme Programming[10] or Scrum.[11] The first value stated in the manifesto favors "individuals and interactions over processes and tools." The *processes* referenced in this first value statement include also agile development processes, which means teams must ensure that their development process supports their needs in the best way possible. Using the principles in the manifesto, teams can find guidance on how to modify and adjust their development processes to best support their needs.

Core Value Pair Statements

The values expressed in the Agile Manifesto apply to all agile projects, superceding guidelines of any specific agile process. The core of the manifesto compares in four statements two values and argues that although each value provides a value in general, the first value is more important than the second

---

[7] See S. Adams, *Dilbert* (http://www.dilbert.com/).

[8] See the Agile Manifesto online: http://agilemanifesto.org.

[9] For an analysis of the Agile Manifesto, see A. Cockburn's *Agile Software Development: The Cooperative Game.* (Reading, Mass.: Addison-Wesley, 2nd edition. 2006). For information on agile development for large projects, see my book *Agile Software Development in the Large*.

[10] For XP, see http://c2.com/cgi/wiki?ExtremeProgrammingRoadmap.

[11] For Scrum, see http://www.controlchaos.com and http://www.scrumalliance.org.

and that the latter half of the each statement is only valid if it supports the former.

Value Pair Statement #1, "Individuals and interactions over processes and tools," highlights the idea that it is always the people involved in a project and how they collaborate that determine a project's success or failure. The manifesto does not devalue processes and tools (otherwise, we wouldn't talk about processes, and the agile community wouldn't have created tools such as unit testing frameworks, integration and configuration management tools, and others), but if individuals don't work together as a team, the best tools and processes won't help the project succeed.

Value Pair Statement #2, "Working software over comprehensive documentation." is perhaps the most often misunderstood of the four statements. People unfamiliar with agile development may mistakenly believe agile projects don't document, or even disdain documentation. Not so. In the same way that processes and tools play a major role in successful development, documentation also plays a major role. However, this value comparison expresses that working software is the critical success factor for any development effort. Documentation might be needed to support or to understand the working software, but it can't and shouldn't be an end in itself .

Value Pair Statement #3, "Customer collaboration over contract negotiation," emphasizes that although you need a contract, it can never be a substitute for a good relationship with your customer. In order to deliver a satisfactory product, involve customers regularly throughout the development process.

Value Pair Statement #4, "Responding to change over following a plan." advocates the importance of reacting to changes (especially in terms of requirements changes), rather than sticking to an inappropriate or obsolete plan. We accept that both the customer and the project team will learn over time, and we want to acknowledge this learning and incorporate it into the development effort. If the finished product delivers what the customer and we planned for before confronting changes and disregards anything we learned during development, the product will be a failure, even if it fulfills a contract.

The agile value system accommodates collocation as well as distributed software development. Later in this chapter, I examine implications of agile principles regarding globally distributed projects.

Systemic Approach

Agile development promotes a systemic approach that is supported by a closed-loop routine of planning, doing (or performing), inspecting (or analyzing), and adapting, as follows:

- In *Planning,* plan immediate activities (having broken down a development project into deliverable chunks, begin planning for the first task). This is most often short-term planning, focusing on the next iteration, but it can also be long term, such as planning the next release.
- In *Doing,* perform activities planned in the first step.
- In *Inspecting,* analyze the performance of the activities planned in the planning step. Did all work as planned? Was there a specific process that worked well and would be appropriate to repeat in the future? Did a specific process or plan fail or require adjustments for the future?
- In *Adapting,* determine what kinds of adjustments the previous inspection step revealed are needed in order to improve development? In this step, decide necessary actions for the following iteration.

The last step in this closed-loop routine provides input for the first step in the next round, and so on.

Risk Reduction

The goal of an agile project is not only to deliver a product at the end of the project's lifetime (also called a deadline), but as well to deliver early and regularly. In order to do so, we divide the project's lifetime into development cycles. A bigger cycle that produces much functionality (sometimes called a feature pack) is called a release. Within that we use a smaller cycle to organize work in smaller chunks, and to deliver smaller functionalities. This smaller cycle is called an iteration.[12] Both a release and iteration lead to a delivery or a potentially shippable product.

---

[12] In Scrum, "an iteration" is called "a sprint." I personally do not like that term because, for me, it connotes frantic, unreserved effort. Iterations should involve adequate resources so that teams are not racing to finish.

A tremendous advantage of agile development is risk reduction through high visibility and transparency. By developing iterations of a working system, receiving regular feedback from the customer and from tests, and with tangible progress, you have access to the actual status of the project. Knowing the actual status of the project in turn enables you to make decisions regarding further deliverables and necessary actions. For example, if you encounter that the system does not fully satisfy the customer and it can't be turned in the right direction, you have the advantage of being able to stop the project early, before all the money has been spent.

The Productivity Myth

Another common, and misguided, argument is that following an agile approach will greatly increase a development team's productivity compared to other approaches. While this can be true, it is not always necessarily so. Agile development guides a team to deliver a working system frequently—"frequently" meaning in iterations lasting one to four weeks. A "working system," on the other hand, is defined by the customer's evaluation of usability. Thus, by providing a working, usable system periodically, say, every two weeks, an agile team ensures maximum business value for its customer.

Therefore, following this approach your customer might decide to go into production with the system earlier. This will give your customer a market advantage. However, it does not necessarily mean that the project as a whole is finished -meaning all required features are implemented- earlier.

More Than Practices

Agility is more than a collection of practices. Every so often, I hear people mixing up specific practices with agility. Practices—for example, Extreme Programming's pair programming or test-driven development—are a great means to preserve the agile value system; however, these practices are not the value system itself. For instance, you can successfully apply pair programming and use a linear (or waterfall) development approach.

Neither Chaotic Nor Undisciplined

Many people consider the agile approach to be an undisciplined approach. Some regard agile as an ad-hoc approach that doesn't require any planning, one in which people act independently according to whim. Sometimes, the agile label is used as an excuse for lack of preparation. For example, if a person has to conduct a workshop or deliver a talk and doesn't prepare material, his or her presentation will consequently follow an ad-hoc approach. This person might argue that the approach used is agile, and therefore doesn't require preparation or planning. Instead, absolutely the opposite is true: Agility requires a lot of planning, even more planning than a linear approach. As Lise B. Hvatum states, "Agile is highly disciplined and more difficult, requires more maturity, than waterfall."[13]

The reality is, agile requires and embraces planning. In agile development, the artifact of a plan is not overly important; the activity of planning, however, is essential. Jakobsen contrasts a choice between an old management style—for example, Taylorism, where managers dictate procedure—and an innovative management style—such as Lean Jidoka[14], based on trust, respect, empowerment, and belief that it is the people who use a process who are best able to improve it.[15]

Improving processes means changing your original plan, and preparing for future re-planning to utilize what you learn as development occurs.

2.3 Agile Principles Influencing Distributed Projects

Listed below are twelve principles of the Agile Manifesto, annotated in terms of their impact on distributed development and direct implementation of an agile approach.

Satisfy the customer through early and continuous delivery of valuable software: Early and continuous delivery is only feasible

---

[13] L.B. Hvatum, personal communication.

[14] Lean Jidoka requires all team members to be responsible for improving the process (immediately) as soon as the quality of the outcome decreases.

[15] C.R. Jakobsen, personal communication.

if all distributed project sites work in concert and take into account customers' wishes.

Welcome changing requirements, even late in development: Communicating requirements changes and their implications requires considerable coordination effort across different sites, but it is not more difficult in a global setting than in a local setting if people on the project are accustomed to pulling together toward a common goal.

Deliver working software frequently: To deliver working software at frequent iterations, the work done by all sites must be carefully integrated. The effort required for teams to deliver a smooth build and integration is considerable even when teams are collocated; it is all the more so for a distributed project.

Business people and developers work together: Regardless of distance between sites, language differences, or cultural disparities, all project members must be fully aware of customer needs, and must make every effort to incorporate customer feedback in the development process.

Trust motivated individuals: Trust generally is built by proximity, a default obstacle in a distributed setting. The sense of closeness, though, must be fostered so as to bind teammates together despite physical distance.

Face-to-face conversation: Because direct, face-to-face conversation is one of the best ways for people to communicate their shared requirements and goals, periodically set aside a time, place, and technology to facilitate effective communication.

Working software is the primary measure of progress: In a distributed setting, making software work over different sites is much more difficult than when everyone is collocated. The major challenge is to ensure the joint effort of the different sites in order not to have several systems but, rather, one coherent, running system in place.

Promote sustainable development: This principle acknowledges the fact that people working too much overtime tend to burn out, adversely affecting the quality of a system. This is true for both distributed and collocated teams, but there is added difficulty on distributed, global projects which have people working at odd or irregular hours in order to communicate and collaborate. The time and physical effort people spend traveling between different sites also can negate their effort to build relationships, making people on distributed projects more susceptible to burn-out than are folks on collocated teams.

Continuous attention to technical excellence and good design: Some projects are negligent in establishing quality assurance at all sites. Assuming that continuous attention to quality is every project's goal, ensure that all sites and all project members work toward attaining it. Additional education may be needed to bring all staff at all sites up to snuff in such areas as testing, refactoring, quality metrics, or other skills.

Simplicity is essential: In distributed settings, project members sometimes develop a general, one-size-fits-all framework for the system in advance of beginning development work because they believe it will ease the developing business functionality later. However, such a framework generally is disconnected from and irrelevant to the customer's actual business requirements and thus doesn't support the domain. Such a framework introduces more complexity and compromises developing business functionality.

Self-organizing teams: Physical distance between sites can be particularly challenging to self-organizing teams because distance makes it harder for people to know and trust one another.[16] So a smell[17] for mistrust is if you're using a more command-and-control style of "collaboration" instead of enable the teams to self-organize. Trust is essential on globally dispersed or distributed teams, whose members may need to be educated about taking responsibility and self-organizing—especially in regard to concepts that contradict their culture.

Team reflection and adjustment: Here is a direct connection to the first value pair of the core of the Agile Manifesto, which values individuals and interactions over processes and tools. At first glance, this is not necessarily different in a distributed setting than it is in a collocated setting: The idea is, allow team members to reflect on how they're progressing to enable them to improve over time. The challenge, however, is to regularly promote reflections across all sites to improve cooperation and federation.

Globally distributed projects face the major challenge of how

---

[16] For more on the concept "trust needs touch," see C. Handy, *Trust and the Virtual Organization* (Boston: Harvard Business Review, 1995), Vol. 73, No. 3, pp. 40-50.

[17] A smell is a sign for or a hint to a problem.

to organize iterations and releases across different sites and still ensure that something functional is delivered at the end of the development cycle. Moreover, the real challenge is not the organization of the work but the integration of the distributed development effort into one working system. Integration and build across teams and sites is essential.

2.4 Summary

There are as many assumptions and misconceptions about global development as there are about agile development. The implications of global development are that several development sites, often spread over several countries, are involved; that development is typically performed by several teams and thus large projects; that even a single team can be distributed across multiple sites (a dispersed team); that multiple companies can be involved; and that customers can be located far away from developers.

Agile development is more than just a specific methodology or collection of defined practices. Culture, values, and beliefs highly influence success in creating trust, collaboration, and a shared vision. One of the significant barriers in distributed projects to overcome is slow feedback due to all types of distances.

3. Building Teams

*It is impossible to create joint plans with people
who strive for different goals.*

— Confucius

The basic idea behind agile development is to provide to the customer, at any point in time, the highest possible business value in terms of working software. Even collocated teams find it challenging to stay focused on this goal, and it is increasingly difficult the more distributed a project is, especially if the global project is very large, with many people working at different sites.

Building a team with a flexible structure is one key to reaching this goal. However, a large distributed project structured as one single team is likely to be neither manageable nor flexible. For a manageable and flexible project, divide staff into subteams, optimally with no more than ten members each.

Typically, distributed projects select a team structure they hope will reduce the channels of communication required between different sites. One approach has been to adopt a traditional linear or waterfall structure, which directs that subteams form based on classical project life-cycle phases, activities or roles such as analysis, design, programming, test, and so on. Following this structured approach, analysts may be located at one site, designers at another, programmers at a third, and so forth.

According to studies reported by Shao and Smith-David,[1] adopting a waterfall approach for distributed software development usually means that each phase is conducted by a specialized team at one location, with phase-associated front-end activities (such as preliminary requirements analysis or conceptual architecture design) and phase-related back-end activities (system test, system deployment, or user-training, for example)

---

[1] B.B.M. Shao and J. Smith-David, op. cit., p. 93.

collocated at the headquarters, whereas mid-life-cycle phase activities (coding, most typically) are transferred "offshore" to a different location. Forming subteams according to activities or phases hinders the collaboration within the whole projects. Moreover, distributing the activities across different sites complicates cross-teamwork for the project.

Another approach to dividing distributed projects into subteams makes technological know-how its guiding principle. Using architectural layers of the software to define team boundaries, people who concentrate, say, on user interfaces form a subteam at one site, database specialists work together at another site, and middleware experts function at a third location. Popular on its own, this approach is often combined with the preceding structuring-along-activities approach.

A possible combination of both structuring approaches would be to locate, say, a team of analysts in England, user-interface specialists in India, and acceptance-test developers in Germany. Given such a structure, it is not surprising how often component interfaces, for example, suffer from compatibility issues, or functionality is developed that does not reflect the customer's requirements. Moreover, finger-pointing between sites becomes commonplace because it's completely unclear whose responsibility it is to develop specific functionality in totality (not just partially). Communication and technological problems such as these can be the result of how teams and subteams are structured, making it difficult for anyone to deliver business value during a project's lifetime, and nigh impossible at the end of the project. Without the valuable customer feedback that delivery of business value triggers, project management and staff cannot learn from the customer in order to successfully adapt the system to the customer's needs.

3.1 Feature Teams

One proven way to maximize the likelihood of delivering business value to the customer is to organize teams according to customer-requested business functionality. As declared in the Agile Manifesto, "The best architectures, requirements, and designs emerge from self-organizing teams."[2]

---

[2] Agile Manifesto online: http://agilemanifesto.org.

That is, instead of building teams according to know-how or system life-cycle phases and activities, organize teams according to their experience in delivering the features the customer wants. With expertise in the required domain and delivery of business value in mind, such teams can be chartered to organize both themselves and their work.

Called feature teams, or domain teams, such teams comprise people who possess or are in the process of acquiring all knowledge and skills necessary to deliver a complete feature that provides business value to the customer. Consequently, a feature team may be staffed by analysts, testers, user interface specialists, database experts, and so on, who work together to deliver the required functionality. Although chosen for their expertise, feature team members do not work solely in their field, but are encouraged to take instruction from feature-team colleagues to learn different roles. Consequently, each feature team "[...]is a generalist in its domain. [...] But although the team consists of these different experts, those experts will not work solely in their field of specialty. Instead, the team members must take different roles."[3] This way, specialized knowledge can be spread to all members of the team, thereby reducing the risk that the project's success will depend on continued involvement of specific experts. Knowledge-sharing enables feature-team members to contribute to each other's work and fosters a shared vision, allowing them to work toward a common objective.

---

[3]For more on my thoughts on feature-team roles, see *Agile Software Development in the Large* (New York: Dorset House Publishing, 2004), pp. 57-58.

Feature Team

Single- and Multi-Site Teams

Organizing a feature team across different sites may seem daunting but can be accomplished in the following, relatively straightforward ways:

- Assemble a *collocated feature team* at one site. This strategy simplifies communication within the team and facilitates synchronization of the shared vision that is necessary in order to achieve the goal of delivering the feature at the end of an iteration. A primary requirement for a collocated feature team is that all required knowledge (or the skills for acquiring this knowledge) is available at the one site. If it is not, either ask people who possess whatever knowledge is missing to impart that knowledge to the collocated feature-team members, or move those people temporarily to the site in order to keep all feature-team members physically together. Note, however, that even with collocated teams, every effort must be made to ensure conceptual integrity (that is, to establish the same look and feel throughout the whole application), among other things.

- A *dispersed feature team* is one that is established across different sites, and is optimal when roles that are needed for the team are not available at a single site and educating people so that they may adopt the roles is not feasible. One drawback can be that internal team synchronization may require a high degree of organizational effort. That notwithstanding, Jamie Allsop reports from his globally dispersed team "[...] that some of our greatest benefits from using an agile methodology where centered around the better utilization of our communication bandwidth. Included in this would also be the rhythmic synchronization at the daily, iteration and release time points".[4] By working on the same set of features while at the same time focusing on delivering business functionality at the end of an iteration, members of a dispersed feature team share and are motivated by a common goal. Individuals grow to work together as a team. For this to work well, individuals on dispersed feature teams need to share common ideals (a topic we'll look more closely at in the next section).

Both types of feature-team structures possess inherent advantages and disadvantages. An advantage of dispersed feature teams is that communication across teams is made easier by the physical proximity of members collocated at the same site, which helps ensure conceptual integrity among myriad feature teams. In all honesty, I was originally surprised to learn that dispersed teams are not always at a disadvantage. For example, setting up a dispersed feature team is advantageous if you are working in a large, distributed setting with many teams. Then, dispersed team members can maintain communication with other collocated project members, even though they belong to other (dispersed or not) feature teams. I recently heard about a project distributed over two locations (The Netherlands and India) that intentionally creates only dispersed teams. The

---

[4]Thanks to Jamie Allsop for sharing this experience.

project's positive experience is based on the reality that project culture unifies and permeates all teams equally. An additional advantage of dispersed feature teams is that the structure "[...] reduces the us- them thinking between the different development sites."[5]

Carefully balance the advantages and disadvantages of collocated and dispersed teams and use a structure that best fits your setting.

Dispersed Teams

Teams accomplish together what individuals cannot accomplish on their own. In order for a feature team to accomplish a task, team members first need to be aware of the fact that they *are* a team, and not several individuals working in common. Together, team members need to do the following:

- *Share a team identity:*[6] Every team member should identify with and feel part of the team.
- *Share a common vision:* Team members need to work toward the same goal.
- *Acknowledge joint responsibility:* Every team member has to commit to sharing responsibility for the work the team promises to deliver.
- *Adhere to collaborative rules and guidelines:* Team members need to have and understand a common protocol that determines how they will work together.
- *Appreciate a joint set of values:* Team members need to agree to what they as a team value (and what they don't value) and use these values to guide their work.

The catch is that no one can instill these characteristics in team members by mere command. Rather, they have to be created, established, and experienced by the team. To achieve this in a timely manner, team members should work together, collocated, for a relatively brief period of time. Collocation provides an artificial environment for members of a dispersed team, yet it

---

[5] My thanks to Bas Vodde for this (personal communication).

[6] For insight into *group* identity, see M.L. Manns and L. Rising, *Fearless Change: Patterns for Introducing New Ideas* (Upper Saddle River, N.J.: Pearson Education, 2005).

still facilitates the process of evolving common rules, guidelines, and an agreed set of values.

Unfortunately, starting with a dispersed team in its *natural* (dispersed) environment will prolong the time it takes team members to gain mutual respect and trust, but the process will focus individuals' attention on the most important challenges they face in their natural environment, thereby creating proximity despite many forms of distance.

Forging a Team

If you are working with a dispersed team, you will have a better chance of establishing a good working relationship among the team members if you enable them to work together, preferably at the beginning of the project. Scott Ambler[7] suggests that in order to help a team jell, members should work together for at least one month; two months would be better. Depending on a team's dispersion, adopt one of the following strategies:

- If the distance between the sites isn't too great (for example, 500 miles or less), team members can travel to the feature team's major site weekly, possibly spending several days each week at the major site. On one of my recent projects, guest workers stayed at a feature team's major site three days a week, a schedule that was feasible because this dispersed subteam was spread between Austria, the Czech Republic, and Hungary, countries that are only a few hours' train ride or brief flight apart.
- If the distance between sites is great, implement a strategy whereby team members work at a host location less frequently but for longer periods of time. This is also known as the concept of expatriates. Imagine a feature team composed of five Chinese and two American developers. A way to help the team jell would be to have the two Americans work for, say, two months in China at the start of the project.

The important thing to remember is that face-to-face meetings are the most effective way to create solidarity and intimacy

[7]S. Ambler, "Bridging the Distance," Dr.Dobb's Portal, http://www.ddj.com/dept/architect/184414899, August 2002.

among team members. McKinney and Whiteside,[8] who conducted a survey of more than two-hundred individuals working in virtual teams, quote one manager regarding dispersed team relationships:

". . . electronic partnerships work extremely well as long as there has been a relationship built in advance."

Building a traditional working relationship between team members before initiating dispersed work increases peer awareness, which in turn motivates individual team members to collaborate actively.[9] Magnus Christerson emphasizes the point, noting, "what and how [teams] work is more important than how long they work. Time is not the critical factor—the critical factor is trust and how long it takes to build. Trust depends not only on people, but also on cultures and values."[10]

Teams Happen by David Hussman[a]

Several years ago, I coached a team "across the pond." As a coach who works in many domains and industries, in many companies and countries, [I find] it can be hard to know what, or who, will be at the next gig. So when asked to coach a "team," I never know what to expect.

As is the case for many of my gigs, the team discussed here was an offshore group, in Ukraine, providing software development services to a U.S.-based management group. The projects were bid on and organized in the U.S., and the requirements were passed on to the developers in Crimea.

When I arrived at the airport, no one was there to meet me as we had discussed. Without knowing much of the language, I was a bit concerned. Then, out of nowhere, a group of friendly faces rolled out of a packed vehicle. This was clearly the team. I immediately felt a team vibe.

Once I was settled in my hotel, we headed to their workspace for our first day together. Upon entering the door to their space, I could again sense the team [spirit]. It was not that

---

[8]V.R. McKinney and M.M. Whiteside, "Maintaining Distributed Relationships," *Communications of the ACM*, Vol. 49, No. 3 (March 2006), pp. 82-86.

[9]For information about team member collaboration, see also B.J. Koh, et al., "Encouraging Participation in Virtual Communities," *Communications of the ACM*, Vol. 50, No. 2 (February 2007), pp. 69-73.

[10]M. Christerson, personal communication.

the space was flowing with *feng shue* or beautiful wall art. Instead, there was a palatable presence of work happening and people working together.

They showed me around and told me about the space. It turned out that more than one of the team [members], and a family helper or two, had built the room and hung the wallboard. They had even built a long U-shaped table where most of the developers sat together each day.

As we worked together, it was clear they were truly a team. They were struggling with problems common for offshore teams. One of many problems was the lack of face-to-face connections with the customers, the kind of connections that help produce better software products in less time.

As an offshore team and part of a newly formed company, the Ukrainians knew they needed to produce. They had been working hard to find various ways to make better connections with the customers and other users, sometimes with success but many times they efforts returned very little.

Around about lunchtime, we all headed to the kitchen. Someone's mother had brought us food and we all sat down to eat a wonderful lunch; the same meal selection was shared by all. The conversations ranged from coding to life, and family. When we finished eating, each developer washed his plate and utensils and put them away. I thought to myself this practice might work well as a team-building exercise for the many large corporate groups who lack any real sense of team, but that is another story.

If there would have been a dishwasher, they would have certainly used it, but there were no issues with doing a bit of plate washing. Everyone knew it was what was needed to keep their house in order and it was not viewed as a huge chore.

As the gig proceeded, I was continually impressed by the way they worked together. Many of the agile value and practices were easy to introduce because of the existing team vibe. The lunchtime experience was only one example of how they kept their team whole. Humor was another, and the need to produce was another.

I did not bring anything that made them a team. They were a team long before my plane landed. What I offered was a set of practices that helped them make better connections within the team and across the pond. Some of the practices we used to help make customer connects were short development cycles, automated acceptance tests, and user stories with personas (short descriptions of people who might use the product and what they value in the product). I am not sure which of the practices were most helpful, but I think the personas truly helped the developers start seeing across the ocean and into the lives and values of their intended audience.

Once we had the personas, we created a collection of user stories with acceptance tests. The tests were another simple and strong way to connect remote developers to product value and improve the iterative output. Instead of hoping that they were producing the right thing, they now had a tool for communicating what would be deemed "done" in a concrete and automated way.

I am not saying that a few personas and automated tests do span the entire Atlantic Ocean, but they do help improve the bandwidth of communication. In this case, they provided a tactic to make connections where there once were none.

I would like to think I did a good job coaching this team. (I was told I did.) As I flew home, I made some notes about the gig. I was surprised how often I typed the word "team." As my sports metaphors are slim, "team" is not a word I often use. I tend to lean more toward "community," as I think it better captures the essence that exists when people bond around creating great products. But the word choice does not matter. For this Ukrainian community, there was that special combination of people; trust, respect, and skills that helped them work with and for each other at the same time. Agile practices did not make them a team, but they did foster the experimentation and learning to find ways to improve.

Remote teams should assume that, to succeed, they needed to embrace iterative development and agility as simple tools that foster collaboration and community. Instead of saying, "How can we practice agile methods," a better question is, "How can agile methods help us succeed?" Agile methods are tools that remote teams or distributed communities need to use to make the connections needed to deliver the right product to its customers.

---

[a]David Hussman (USA), Software Anthropologist and Agile

Coach, devjam.com

3.2 Roles

To be fully functional throughout a project's life cycle, a feature team typically requires that a variety of roles be performed. For each role described below, the person or people responsible for performing it will be most effective if they are able to travel to the different teams, as needed. Direct, face-to-face communication allows role-players to gain a comprehensive understanding of project progress and ensures that key information is not only communicated well, but is also understood by all other members of the team.

There are several basic premises that pertain to feature-team roles, as follows: Most roles need not be fulfilled by one person for the duration of the project; most role-players can assume several roles as time and rationale permit; one role rarely equates exactly to one person's responsibility. Determining and mapping roles and people's responsibilities depends on such factors as the qualified people at hand, their knowledge of the risk implied by the system being built (for instance, their familiarity with specific technologies and the business domain), and the size and distribution of a team.

Feature-Team Constellation

The baseline of operational feature teams is that they either already comprehend or are capable of acquiring required knowledge to complete a unit of business functionality. In addition to each individual's domain and technical know-how, a team must be able to *deliver* functionality. Thus, feature teams typically need to include all or most of the following roles:

- *Architect:* ensures the conceptual integrity of the system (a topic we'll look more closely at in the next section).
- *Database administrator:* maintains databases.

- *Designer:* conceives and directs a coherent design of required features.
- *Documenter:* provides necessary documentation for developed features.
- *Domain expert:* helps teammates to understand the domain.
- *Infrastructure specialist:* ensures that the development environment is working and supportive.
- *Integration expert:* possesses the know-how to integrate, build, deliver, and deploy a feature within the whole system, and ensures a working configuration management.
- *Programmer:* codes the required functionality as well as accompanying unit tests.
- *Tester:* works closely with the domain expert to define acceptance criteria for business functionality. Tests the feature in terms if they can be accepted.
- *User interface designer:* knows how the user interface should appear and feel, and then creates it accordingly.

In many of my projects, the whole feature team shares the responsibility for each role. This means that any feature-team member will take on any role when needed. We seldom have people dedicated to fulfilling only one of these roles. To refer to all these required roles, we typically use the general term "developer." The number of people on a feature team varies, but I recommend that there be seldom fewer than three members and never more than ten. A good rule to follow for team size is the Miller rule of seven, plus or minus two. Sangwan, et al., further recommend that "[…]no team should be larger than ten staff members, and no single development site should have more than 100 engineers (or ten teams of 10)."[11]

Sometimes, if a feature requires a special technology or connectivity, a project will require temporary assistance from specialists gathered from outside of the feature team. When this happens, I recommend that the experts become a member of the feature team within a given timeframe (for example, one iteration). This may require that the experts travel to the site where the feature resides. Such experts don't stay with a specific feature team for the whole project but instead work as needed to support a specific feature team.

---

[11]R. Sangwan, et al., *Global Software Development Handbook* (New York: Auerbach, 2007), p. 97.

Establish a similar relationship between a mentor/trainer and a feature team requiring support or specific knowledge: Mentors work with a team for as long as necessary to transfer the knowledge. This may mean a mentor travels to a remote feature team or to several sites to train members of a dispersed team. Efficiency and effectiveness depend upon working together in-person with mentors. Avoid the monopolization of knowledge—that is, a situation in which a few elites are regarded as irreplaceable experts. Monopolization presents a big risk in that, just like everyone else, experts take vacation, become sick, change jobs, and so on, leaving behind a project in limbo.

If possible, I recommend that team members stay together within a feature team over the whole lifetime of the project. The biggest benefit is that a team can build its identity and, once it establishes communication paths, knowledge and conversation typically flow more easily during the rest of the collaboration. Dispersed as well as collocated feature teams can reap these benefits.

Architect and Chief Architect

The architect's main task is to ensure conceptual integrity, independent of the number of feature teams or sites involved. Brooks defines conceptual integrity as follows:[12]

"Every part must reflect the same philosophies and the same balancing of desiderata. Every part must even use the same techniques in syntax and analogous notions in semantics. Ease of use, then, dictates unity of design, conceptual integrity."

Only conceptual integrity enables simplicity—and simplicity in turn enables maintainability. In my experience, "[o]n a typical agile project with a small team, you will often end up without an architectural lead because the whole team is of equal value and takes the same responsibility for the whole project. Although this could or should be a goal for a large team, too, it would never work, because development would diverge, uncoordinated".[13]

This is one reason why the architect's role is so important. In a project with only one collocated team, this whole team can take

---

[12] F.P. Brooks, Jr., *The Mythical Man-Month: Essays on Software Engineering*, 20th anniv. ed. (Reading, Mass.: Addison-Wesley, 1995), p. 44.

[13] See Eckstein, op. cit., p. 127.

responsibility for conceptual integrity. In some projects (still not too big), it might be enough that an experienced developer additionally takes the role of the architect. Depending on the technology used, the content of the project, and project size, the demand regarding the architect's role varies:

- *One project architect:* The one architect oversees/advises all technical decisions and acts also as the major contact for the (lead) product owner in order to learn about technical dependencies between features.
- *One architect per feature team:* If the project is rather complex and unknown, one architect *per feature team* is needed. However, once the team has gained necessary knowledge and experience, it may only need one or a few architects for the whole project. The position of architect on a feature team is rarely full-time, but rather may be an additional role adopted by a developer.
- *One-to-n architects to support all teams:* If you have fewer architects than feature teams, each architect should work with a single feature team for a limited period of time (for example, for one iteration) before moving on to support another feature team.

No matter if you have an architect for every feature team or a group of architects supporting many feature teams, it is important that all architects communicate, and one chief—or lead—architect pulls the strings and ensures they work toward the same project vision. Otherwise, it is very likely that every team or every site, or both, will make its own architectural decisions that will probably differ from one to another. The main responsibility of the chief architect is to ensure that the big picture (from a technical viewpoint) is understood by everybody on the team. The architectural lead should also train the team members by helping them, for example, to see the big picture and to take responsibility. So, the lead architect will not only be the one memorizing the key ideas but, more importantly, the one who spreads these ideas so that more and more people will have the same understanding of the system.[14]

Spreading these ideas and helping the other team members to see the big picture does not refer to concepts only, but rather to the actual system. Thus, the chief architect does not just create,

---

[14]Ibid., op. cit., pp. 128-29.

say, documents; he or she may also code. No matter whether a project has a single architect, several architects, or even one architect per feature team, architects must always work with the feature teams and understand that they provide a service for the feature teams.

Another important lesson to learn is that the worst architectures are often the result of democratic decisions. I don't mean that the chief architect should dictate architectural decisions; rather, he ensures that all opinions are heard and, if required, evaluates before a final decision is made. It is a chief architect's responsibility to ensure that all architects accept and respect that final decision. Final agreement on a decision is key to success. In order to accomplish this, I recommend you follow the process of *nemawashi,* noted in *The Toyota Way:*[15]

"Make decisions slowly by consensus, thoroughly considering all options; implement rapidly."

The basis for this process is that every party gets a fair hearing and is allowed to provide input, and is therefore involved in the decision-making. Ultimately, this ensures that all participants can agree with the decision and prioritize their own objectives below the project's objectives.

Experiences as a Software Architect in Global Agile Projects by Michael Kircher[a]

In my roles as architect—in this concrete case, as lead architect of a mid-size development project (about 50 developers)—I have been able to gather experiences regarding the scalability of the role of software architect in an agile project.

The project concerned the development of two subsystems: an embedded device to be integrated in vehicles, and an enterprise-scale information system, laid out as a three-tier system combined with batch processing. In this setting, we had multiple challenges. First, three development locations in Europe were involved. Second, the developed software was expected to be reused as a platform for similar solutions, with similar requirements, after the first project was completed. Third, the requirements were not fixed: The customer—represented by a product owner—was elaborating the key use cases as development continued.

---

[15]J.K. Liker, op. cit., p. 241.

For me, these challenges meant that I needed a way to constantly evolve the architecture on multiple sites while ensuring minimal complexity in order to secure later reuse. In my experience, this is a very typical problem description for a software architect in a global and agile software development project.

****

A brief note on what software architecture is concerned with: Architecture, in my understanding, concerns everything that is expensive to change afterward, so it concerns not only the global structure of the software but also the employed technologies, decisions for internationalization support, and the like. With this interpretation of architecture, it is easy to see that architecture matters in agile projects. The key difference in an agile project is that the specific architecture evolves during the project instead of remaining as planned in advance through to the project's very end. Maybe a good analogy is to compare between *static and up-front-designed architecture* and *dynamic, constantly maturing architecture*. This is not to say that everything changes in the latter case; far from it. Elementary design decisions, such as layering, partitioning principles, and programming idioms, stay the same, most likely including the initial architectural style, such as Broker, Common Repository, and Pipes & Filters.

****

Due to the multiple subsystems and development sites involved on this project, it was obvious that a single architect was not sufficient. We established an architect for every major subsystem and site—which correlated as we tried to avoid splits across sites within a subsystem—coached and guided by me, the lead architect. This orchestration of architect roles allowed the handling of situations that required hard and final decisions. The general strategy is to have one lead architect and subordinate software architects, partitioned according to boundaries of subsystems, problem domains—such as technical architecture (infrastructure) and business (domain) logic—and especially sites.

Concerning the focus and priorities of a software architect, I have a very dedicated opinion: A software architect must ensure, in decreasing order of priority: 1) consistency among design decisions and the resulting architecture, 2) communication among developers and with stakeholders, 3) guidance regarding best-practice in daily design decisions of the team, and, 4) making design decisions. This last point might seem contrary to what many believe, because many expect the architect to make *all* design decisions by herself or himself. In my experience, that is actually the *worst* you could do because of many reasons, the topmost being that developers are not committed to dictated decisions and that the number of required decisions will flood the architect, hence hampering project progress as the architect becomes a bottleneck. The role of the architect can only scale and architects can only maintain control over design decisions if they remove themselves from actual design work and, instead, install themselves as a control, reviewing relevant decisions before implementation. Thus, architects should guide teams to employ wise design practice.

Coming back to agility: The concept of software architects coaching and distributing responsibility aligns quite naturally with the principles of agility, with empowered teams that are aligned to accomplish common goals.

[a]Michael Kircher (Germany), Director syngo Platform Development, Siemens Healthcare, formerly Principal Engineer, Siemens Corporate Technology

Coach

Every feature team needs a coach, a spokesperson (in Scrum, called the Scrum Master) to ensure that the team is able to do its work. This doesn't mean that team members cannot take responsibility for resolving matters if there is something in their way (they can), but rather that, in order to move the project forward, there is someone who cares for their issues and who will take problems to the right people. The coach serves also as a firewall or gatekeeper for the team, so that team members won't always be interrupted if someone from outside has a question or request.[16]

---

[16]For more on firewalls and gatekeepers, see J.O. Coplien and N.B. Harrison, *Organizational Patterns of Agile Software Development* (Englewood Cliffs, N.J.: Prentice-Hall, 2004).

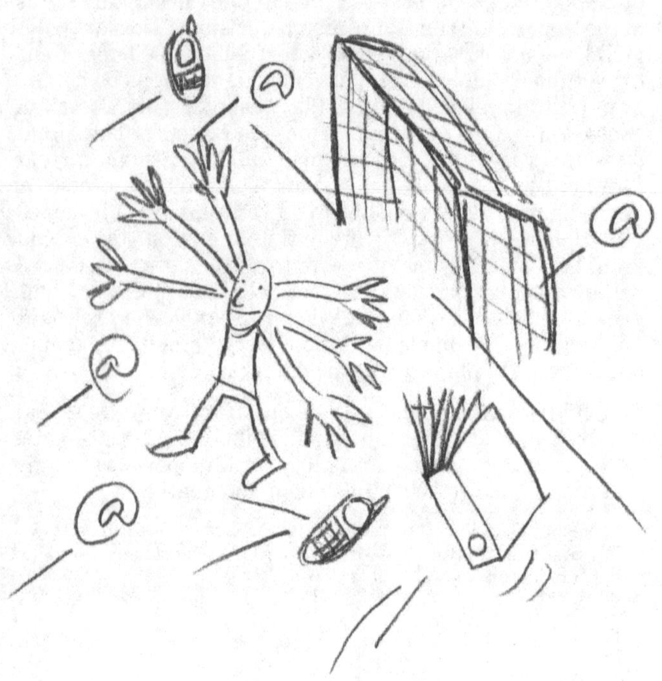

Gatekeeper

Additionally, the coach ensures the location and scheduling of team meetings. This doesn't necessarily mean that the coach personally reserves a conference room, the responsibility should be shared among all team members, but merely makes certain that this type of task is done. A coach also helps team members stay organized and current. For example, he or she may remind team members to verify that a particular agreement is valid, and that if outdated or invalid, it be either eliminated or replaced.

A large distributed project will have several coaches, typically one for each feature team. I find it most effective when a coach is actually a member of the team (avoid, for example, selecting team members' managers) and is collocated with the team. A coach should have an additional role such as developer (the most common case), or tester. However, depending on whether or not team members work smoothly together, the coach may have to defer, say, a development task if too busy fulfilling the job of coach. If the team is dispersed, the coach must maintain adequate contact with *all* team members (by phone and e-mail, and by traveling to their work sites).

Product Owner and Product Manager

Feature-team members need to know which feature needs to be implemented next and whom to ask if they have problems understanding the requirements for the feature. In order to satisfy the customer, the Agile Manifesto stresses, "Business people and developers must work together daily throughout the project."[17]

Not every feature team, nor every customer, can afford to move in together—nor is such a drastic effort necessary. Basically, a feature team needs somebody who represents the customer in a role that often is simply referred to as "the customer" (in XP, called the onsite-customer). However, although this role could be filled by an actual customer, it is more often appropriate that the person just represent the customers' perspective (but isn't a customer himself). Having someone represent the customers' perspective is especially helpful if the system will have to serve customers who have differing opinions regarding the future functionality of the system. To differentiate between the real customer and the role-player representing the customers' perspective, some use the label "product manager," or "proxy customer," but I like the Scrum term "product owner" for this role.

The product owner clarifies and assigns priority to the different requirements of all the various customers. In order to do so, the product owner needs thorough knowledge of the customer's business domain, and moreover, an effective communication channel to the different customers. As Magnus Christerson emphasizes: "Product owners/managers need to spend quality time with real customers continuously. I used to have the guideline that 25% of the time of a product manager should be spent on direct customer activities."[18]

Product owners on my projects generally come from different areas or departments within the company sponsoring the

---

[17]Agile Manifesto online: http://agilemanifesto.org/principles.html.

[18]M. Christerson, personal communication.

project. People with a background, say, in marketing, customer support, product management, sales, or business analysis are good candidates. My general rule of thumb is: The person selected must be someone with insight into the customers' domain. Thus, if building a product for developers, a developer is a good candidate to place in the role of the product owner. Who is best qualified depends very much on the system to be built. If several different types of customer need to be served, the product owner's task can be especially demanding. Balancing and assigning priority to the different needs of diverse customers and drawing conclusions from them are major responsibilities of the product owner.

If the system being built is highly complex or the team is not particularly well versed in the customer's business domain, one product owner might only be able to support one feature team. In some of my projects, one product owner was able to support up to three teams; in other projects, we needed one product owner per feature team. Generally, the role of product owner is very demanding! Thus, it is essential to ensure that he or she does not get burned-out, caught between the feature team requesting support regarding business knowledge and the real customer whose needs must be met. One way to maintain sanity is to establish a support structure along the following lines:

- *Product-owner team:* On a large project, it often is not sufficient to just have *one* product owner because the required tasks are too extensive for one person, but instead to have a team of product owners, each of whom may be able to support one to three feature teams.
- *Lead product owner:* A team of product owners will need at its head a lead product owner to serve as arbiter and final decision-maker in the event of disagreement. The lead product owner's major responsibility is to make priority decisions based on input from customers as well as from the team of product owners. In the same way that the chief architect pulls the strings regarding technical decisions, the lead product owner retains final judgment for business decisions. Depending on the complexity of the system and the project, the lead product owner may have no task other than coordinating the team of product owners and keeping in touch with customers. In most cases, however, a lead product owner also can fulfill the role of a regular product owner, steering one feature team and serving as

lead product owner in parallel.

Although responsibility for the mother-lode of customer contact belongs to the lead product owner, the other members of the product-owners team need to work with customers in addition to supporting their feature teams. Ideally, product owners are collocated with the feature team or teams they support, and travel to customer sites to get and give feedback and to clarify possible misunderstandings.

The more "business complexity" there is on the project, the closer the product owner should be to the team. Product owners who support one or more dispersed feature teams, of course, will need to travel frequently to the sites involved. At times when the product owner can not be collocated with his feature team communication can be effectively maintained with off-site contacts and teams by using all kinds of communication media to connect and enrich the feature team's and product owner's conversation. Although not always feasible, product owners should strive to limit the time when they are not collocated with their feature team.

The role of the product owner is the same whether working with an onshore or offshore team. I want to emphasize this point because I every so often hear people state that offshore teams will not have a collocated product owner, gaining access to their product owner only at the project's base location. After all, agility is about focusing on business value and, therefore, it is relatively unimportant where feature teams are located. Every feature team will benefit most from direct support from the business side and thus will always function best if it has the support of a collocated product owner. Matt Simon, project manager for ThoughtWorks advices: "Assuming that your offshore team is unable to locate a business customer willing to play the role of the onsite customer, you'll have to establish some type of proxy customer."[19]

If there is no direct contact between the product owner and "his" feature team, you need a different product owner – the idea of a product owner is actually to reduce the miscommunication between development and the customer. If you don't acknowledge this you're just introducing another layer of indirection

---

[19]M. Simon, "Internationally Agile," *Informit.com*, http://www.informit.com/articles/article.asp?p-25929, March 2002.

between the team and the customer and miscommunication will be nurtured all the more.

Direct Connection

Project Manager

Several agilists claim that agile projects have evolved and no longer require the role of the project manager. Most traditional agile teams and certainly large and distributed teams, however, stumble without assigning responsibility for project-critical factors such as the following:

- *Politics:* In my experience, the project manager's most important task is to deal with organizational politics. Typically, a project needs support both from inside and outside the company. Establishing and preserving that support is very often a full-time job.
- *Personnel issues:* The project manager should be the knowledgeable and helpful face of human resources for the team, having insight into team pressures and personal problems, giving leeway, say, on personal days and holidays while supporting the team as a whole. Often, the project manager is the one who can solve tough problems that the team coach cannot solve by virtue of being too close to the team or not close enough to company politics.
- *Budgetary control:* The project manager typically is responsible for controlling the budget and providing relevant information to the product owners or the lead product

owner. In smaller and less complex projects, this responsibility is and should be in the hands of the (lead) product owner.

- *Hiring:* Project managers usually are also responsible for organizing the search for skilled people based on a project team's input.

The project manager ensures that all project members can do their job so that the project can progress, and, depending on the actual size of the team, several people may be needed to support the project manager fulfilling these tasks.

For a distributed project development team spread across several sites, where the project manager actually is located is comparatively unimportant. He or she will have to travel to all project team locations. However, avoid locating all development in one place and all project management in another. Project management that is not skillfully integrated with the development effort simply amounts to no project management at all: developers will lack context with which to complete project goals. As Ed Yourdon observes, ". . . the main thing is that the project manager *and* the rest of the team are from the same organization, part of the same culture, and presumably acquainted with one another already."[20]

Collocate Key Roles with Teams

All the responsibilities discussed above, whether formally assigned to an architect, coach, product owner, or project manager, are integral to agile development. I want to reiterate that these key roles function most efficiently and effectively when collocated with their respective team or teams. In fact, each is part of the team.

Every so often, I am surprised by the tendency in some organizations to assign the key roles to project members located at project headquarters. This practice is not really helpful. In order to support their feature teams adequately the key roles have to be (physically) close to their teams.

Having noted that, there is one exception: When a feature team is dispersed and, consequently, there is no single site where

---

[20]E. Yourdon, *Outsource: Competing in the Global Productivity Race* (Englewood Cliffs, N.J.: Prentice-Hall, 2005), p. 56.

it is located, then there is no specific site where key roles should be located. It then becomes extremely important that people fulfilling these key roles are willing and able to travel (most probably, a lot) to all sites involved, and that they have particularly good communication skills in a dispersed setting.

3.3 Ensuring Conceptual Integrity

Correlating the efforts of feature teams will ensure focus on the highest business value in a given system. Without an architect, feature teams may grow near-sighted and focus on features rather than on cross-features like conceptual integrity. Avoid ending up with a system consisting of a hodgepodge of looks and feels, diverse database access, and the like. Conceptual integrity is the basis for a maintainable system. Only this allows a simple vision to evolve which facilitates the general understanding of the system as well as future upkeep and changes. This is also required by the Agile Manifesto declaration of architectural philosophy:

> "Simplicity—the art of maximizing the amount of work not done—is essential."[21]

For every system, and even more so for large systems, simplicity comes from conceptual integrity. Architects are responsible for conceptual integrity. Depending on the size of the project, as well as on the complexity of it, it could be enough to just have one architect or it might be necessary to have a team of architects in place to ensure conceptual integrity.

Starting Team Provides Model

If you have started a project with just one team and this team implements two to three key use cases together with a referential implementation of the architecture, this might already be sufficient to establish conceptual integrity. Referential implementation will act as a role model for all further development, serving as an example on which to expand the system and as

---

[21] Agile Manifesto online: http://agilemanifesto.org/principles.html.

a basis for learning more about the business domain and the technology.[22]

Moreover, if you have carefully built this starting team (that is selecting people from all sites involved), then all sites will learn from it, and knowledge about cross-functional issues will spread across sites.

Technical Service Team

If the complexity and the size of the project make it impossible for the group of architects to maintain conceptual integrity, think about establishing a separate team to provide this support. For example, if the system you are building consists of a complex user interface, you might need to establish a separate team, called a *technical service team,* that is tasked with creating the infrastructure or a framework for it. This strategy allows feature teams to more easily build user interfaces. Another reason to form a technical service team is to build different products based on the same architecture. Thus the technical service team will provide the foundation so that the feature teams can build their features on top of it using the same concepts.

Key to success for a technical service team is that the work it delivers is a real service for the feature teams. This means that the technical service team understands that the feature teams are the "customers" stating the requirements. It is not the technical service team that comes up with ideas independent of their customers' needs (although I have seen the latter far too often). No, it is that technical service teams should always regard themselves as pure service providers for the feature teams.[23]

Feature teams in turn then have to act as customers and must additionally provide a "product owner" for the technical service team. This product owner prioritizes and steers technical-service-team development. The major difference for feature teams is that the customers of a technical service team are also developers, so that the "features" a technical service team provides are technical and not business features. Even the technical features are driven by business features, because the

---

[22] For more on the topic of referential implementation, see Eckstein, op. cit., p. 114.

[23] Ibid., op. cit., p. 53.

feature teams will still direct their efforts toward developing business functionality.

If the technical service team provides the architecture for different products, the same holds true. That is, the teams that develop these products are the customers for the technical service team, and they state the requirements.

3.4 Summary

The most important part of building a team is to ensure that the team is able to deliver a discrete project goal, a whole feature. Charge a whole team responsible for a whole business feature to keep clear where ownership lies if, for instance, towards the end of an iteration, not all tasks are completed. Then, it is the team members' job to work together and finish that feature. Still, in order to deliver a coherent system, conceptual integrity has to be ensured as well. This is the task of the architect(s) and, depending on the project, possibly also of the technical service team.

You might need to balance physical proximity with the need for specific skills and roles within a team by setting up a dispersed feature team. It is very important for dispersed teams to have a common goal, which is the focus on the features they're responsible for developing, as well allowing time for members to create a team identity so they work effectively together.

In contrary to dispersed feature teams, with collocated feature teams you need to focus more on the cross-team communication between the different sites for enforcing the big picture and common goal of the whole project. Often, in our projects we end up with some teams being collocated and others being dispersed.

There are three central roles for ensuring the big picture:

- The (lead) product owner, who provides the business perspective
- The (chief) architect who ensures the technical vision on the product
- The project manager, who supports the organizational side.

In a study of several distributed projects, Biehl summarizes lessons learned from managers who had been responsible for unsuccessful distributed development projects: "... they had neglected three critical factors: not using cross-functional teams; not engaging in cross-functional communication; and not bringing end users on board early enough during the project."[24]

The architecture has to be a service for feature teams and therefore take the latter's requirements into account. This is the case regardless of whether the intent is to ensure conceptual integrity with one architect, with a team of architects, or with one or several technical service teams. Every person involved has to support this approach to the same extent.

---

[24]M. Biehl, "Success Factors for Implementing Global Information Systems," *Communications of the ACM,* Vol. 50, No. 1 (January 2007), p. 57.

4. Establishing Communication and Trust

Trust,
which is shared amongst new friends,
is created step-wise.

— Johann Wolfgang von Goethe

Agile development's success on a global scale depends partially on a project's ability to establish and cultivate strong communication channels among distributed and dispersed groups. Some experts maintain that methods that are fundamental to agility won't work in a distributed environment because of the great amount of communication they require. Sakthivel, for example, assesses the feasibility of using iterative and incremental approaches on global projects:

"Due to their high task dependencies and required face-to-face interaction with users during their iterative analysis, design, and trial stages, they are not suitable for mid- and large-size offshore projects."[1]

It is my view, however, that rather than *requiring* an inordinate amount of communication, agile development embraces communication as *enabling* people to collaborate and trust each other. Emphasis on the value of strong channels for communication to facilitate collaboration and trust is as well true for distributed teams as for small, collocated teams. As Carmel puts it,

"Creating an effective global team from multiple sites involves several key success factors: building trust, encouraging open communication, building personal relationships, and bridging cultural differences."[2]

---

[1] S. Sakthivel, "Managing Risk in Offshore Systems Development," *Communications of the ACM,* Vol. 50, No. 4 (April 2007), p. 71.

[2] Carmel, op. cit., p. 82.

I've made the point in preceding chapters that, in order to succeed as a team, team members need a common vision, joint rules, and shared values. Members of a feature team can achieve these goals with relative ease, but it takes considerable effort to ensure that all individuals and all teams at all sites across the whole project develop mutual respect and trust to work together successfully.

4.1 Trust and Mutual Respect

Trust cannot be commanded and takes time to establish, especially in a distributed environment. Built by open, honest, and reliable communication, trust is difficult—and in some settings impossible—to build without the parties meeting face-to-face. Once built, maintaining trust requires work. Pugh sums up the delicate balance with a dose of reality: "Trust is developed incrementally, broken precipitously."[3]

The concept of developing trust incrementally is based on a team-psychosocial-development model explored in psychological literature in the 1960s.[4] The model examines four stages individuals in a group go through to become a team: *forming* (getting together and defining objectives), *storming* (first conflicts with consequences on roles), *norming* (accepting rules and developing guidelines), and *performing* (working toward a common goal and constructive resolution of conflicts). Going through all four stages can take a global team as long as three months.

In order to create mutual respect, every project member must regard others as colleagues and not as cheap laborers. As promoted in the Agile Manifesto, trust must accompany team preparation during development: "Build projects around motivated individuals. Give them the environment and support they need, and trust them to get the job done."[5]

---

[3]K. Pugh, "Managing Distributed and Global Teams" *Proceedings of the Software Best Practices Conference, 2007* (Boston, 2007).

[4]B. Tuckman, "Developmental Sequence in Small Groups," *Psychological Bulletin*, Vol. 63 (1965), pp. 384-89.

[5]Agile Manifesto online: http://agilemanifesto.org/principles.html.

Mutual Trust

Trust Threshold

A communication channel for building a trusting relationship must be established with regular—and, at the beginning, frequent, face-to-face meetings. In my own and several colleagues' experience, the frequency of in-person meetings can taper to eight to twelve weeks after the trusting relationship has been established. We have found, however, that waiting longer than eight to twelve weeks can drive people close to what is called the communication and trust threshold, beyond which risks such as the following abound:

- The relationship is completely broken.
- Communication, ineffective at best, fails.
- The whole team feels stress as it struggles to recover the trusting relationship.

Whenever the communication and trust threshold looms near or is crossed, teams must start repairing the damage, which may require that multiple in-person meetings be conducted before the trusting relationship can be re-established. How much time can elapse between face-to-face meetings before the communication and trust threshold is breached depends on the quality of the initially established relationship as well as on the duration of the in-person meetings. I find that when people spend a single day working face-to-face, the communication and trust threshold comes at about eight weeks. If people meet face-to-face for a whole iteration, the communication and trust threshold will take longer to establish. You have probably experienced this threshold as well in your private life. There are good friends, if you haven't seen them for five years, you catch up right at the spot where you lost sight of each other. And there are other (putative) good friends, if you don't see them for a while you have problems finding a topic to talk about and it just doesn't feel like a good relationship anymore. So the communication and trust threshold very much depends on the quality of the once established relationship.

One additional caveat: Whenever team members are brought together, whether as members of a distributed team or from multiple teams on a project, it is imperative to preserving trust that all participants show complete respect for everyone else.

Changing Meeting Locations

If a team comprises many members who must work effectively as a big group or the cost of travel is prohibitive, each team or site may elect to send one or two representatives, rotating representatives so that each attendees a subset of meetings. If only the same representatives go to each meeting, a "head monopoly" regarding knowledge as well as social contacts may develop that may be difficult to overcome. Furthermore, information, culture, and joint project values will spread more easily if as many team members as possible experience some in-person meetings.

If team members always will gather at one location, no matter whether as members of the whole project or just one of the dispersed teams, meeting locations should alternate between all involved sites. This way, everyone can experience the responsibility of hosting a meeting, including the benefits of being at home during the event. In the same way, everyone also experiences visiting different sites and the excitement (and hassle) of travel.

Many distributed projects require that all team members, from time to time, travel to the project's main site for face-to-face meetings. This practice becomes completely unreasonable and ill-advised if such meetings *always* take place at the main site, giving dispersed team members the trust-busting message that the main site is actually centrally coordinating (or dominating) all sites.[6]

Alternately changing the meeting location is one way of showing respect for all sites and team members involved.

Vocabulary

All members of the whole team need to be sensitive to the vocabulary used for project work. Using terms that might only be familiar to the most-experienced technical staff can damage communication efforts and trust-building. It is fact that some technical terms mean different things at different places while other terms are troublesome in a global setting. Several terms that can be confusing on global projects follow:

- *Nightly build* typically refers to one build per day, performed during the night; however, in a global environment, it is unclear to whose night we refer.
- *Morning roll call* typically refers to a feature-driven development team's daily synchronization effort. As with the previous term, it is unclear whose "morning" is meant. Terms like *daily synchronization* and Scrum's *Daily Scrum* are similarly used and also suffer from the same lack of clarity about whose "day" is in focus.
- *Remote site* typically refers to a location distant to the main site, possibly even to the listener's site. As such a person undoubtedly would not consider the site the least bit remote, it is unclear which site is meant.

In order to address different local meanings of terms (an issue even when people at different locations speak the same native tongue, for instance in United Kingdom and the United States), I recommend that project members create a glossary on a project-internal wiki[7] to capture their linguistic differences. A glossary won't completely eliminate misunderstandings, but it can alert people throughout the whole project to possible misunderstandings.

---

[6] I discuss central coordination versus global integration in detail in Chapter 2, "Assessing Agility and Distributed Projects."

[7] A Wiki is a web based collaboration plattform, which allows to work jointly on HTML documents (see also Leuf, Bo and Cunningham, Ward: The Wiki Way: Collaboration and Sharing on the Internet. Addison-Wesley. 2001.

4.2 Communication

Investing effort in communication is the definitive challenge of distributed development—and it is often ignored. The Agile Manifesto highlights the importance of face-to-face communication: "The most efficient and effective method of conveying information to and within a development team is face-to-face conversation."[8]

One colleague of mine reported that his company stopped global development after ten years, having found that the practice was only beneficial when performed by a whole team together at one location. When teams worked in a distributed setting, communication failed and projects failed, clearly demonstrating the importance of communication to a project's success.

In-Person Team Meetings

Establishing a trusting relationship requires that team members meet in person from time to time. As Koh, et al., observe, "a lack of social presence creates communication weakness in any virtual community. ...Social presence ... is critical for effective communications in many social/work contexts."[9] There are different approaches for accomplishing this, depending on distance between sites:

- More and longer in-person meetings are conducted at the beginning of the collaboration and less frequent ones as time goes by. Often, a project starts with an in-person kick-off meeting followed by one or two iterations during which people work together at one site. Thereafter, team members only meet on special occasions (for example, to attend a specific workshop or to release an increment of the product).
- Feature-team members meet a couple of days every week, a practice that works best if the distance between sites is not too great (for example, team members from, say, the Czech Republic might work in Austria two days every week, as on one of my projects).

[8]Agile Manifesto online: http://agilemanifesto.org/principles.html.
[9]B.J. Koh, et al., op. cit., p. 70.

- Dispersed-team members rotate between different sites (for example, a Finnish-Japanese project on which ten Japanese went to Finland and four Finns worked in Japan, with rotations lasting about three months each[10]).
- Team members meet frequently for regular events (for example, dispersed feature-team members meet in person for each iteration review and planning).

The dispersed team should make sure to select a different location for each in-person meeting, so that each team member sometimes get to stay at his home location.

Face-to-Face Project Meetings

In order to avoid breaching the threshold for trusted connections, project members of the whole team and not only of a feature team need to meet face-to-face from time to time. Whereas in-person team meetings focus on interests and concerns of a single feature team, the face-to-face project meeting concentrates on superior project needs. If a project can package iterations into releases, the releases can serve as goal-markers for face-to-face meetings[11]. By setting up a physical get-together, say, at the end of every third iteration or at the end of each release having a relatively short timescale, project members preserve both communication channels and trusting relationships.

As for other face-to-face meetings, also for the whole project team meeting, you should ensure to not meet at the same location all the time. Instead for enforcing mutual understanding and respect, it is a good idea to change the meeting location using a round robin strategy across all sites involved.

Your project might be too big for bringing actually all project team members together. I suggest inviting only one to two representatives from every feature team. You should ensure that for the next face-to-face project meeting other persons will represent their feature team. This way everyone will experience the get-together. Depending on the kind of the meeting you need to ensure that the product owners will attend the meeting as well.

---

[10]For an overview of this exchange, see Carmel, op. cit., p. 158.

[11]I discuss release planning in detail in chapter 7 "Ensuring Business Value".

Again depending on the actual size of the team, you might consider to invite all project members from the host site and only the representatives from the sites that need to travel. By changing the hosting site with every face-to-face project meeting, all team members will be able to attend the project meeting at least at one point in time (at their home site).

People Rotation

Rather than bringing the whole team together for in-person team or face-to-face project meetings, another viable option is to schedule subsets of staff members to change places to work at different sites[12]. This exchange must take all sites into account, ensuring that it is not only team members from foreign sites who are asked to travel and work at the main site. In addition, people who rotate among sites should not all be executives, but rather must be all types of team members. It is important that people from all sites work at all other sites for at least one exchange. An additional benefit of this practice is that it helps team members gain a better understanding of the problems different sites have to tackle.

Jepsen emphasizes the point that rotating team members help both to seed and maintain relationships, and further observes that such rotations should last for weeks rather than days so that rotating team members can maximize the experience.[13] In my experience, rotations are best made when they last months or, at the least, reflect a specific iteration schedule.

In order to make such exchanges a beneficial experience for all parties, all sites must prepare to accommodate people from other locations. For example, sites may need to organize extra office space and an environment that makes it easy for visitors to acclimate and start working. Staff members as well as managers at host sites need to plan ways to help visiting team members integrate socially as well as to help them learn about cultural, legal, and bureaucratic differences. For example, people need to be aware that different countries have different regulations regarding, say, work visas or how long visitors may work before they have to pay non-resident taxes.

---

[12]I discuss this in more detail in "Forging a Team" in chapter 3, "Building Teams".

[13]O. Jepsen, "Agile Meets Offshore: How Can Agile Practices Help in Offshore Projects?" *Proceedings of the Agile 2006 Conference* (Minneapolis, Minn.: July 2006).

Communication Costs

Communicating at in-person team and face-to-face project meetings implies cost—in many areas, but especially in terms of travel and time—but there is unfortunately no way around it. As Pugh observes, "You will pay the costs of a face-to-face meeting, regardless of whether you have one or not. Not having one may cost more."[14] Before setting off to participate in face-to-face team and in-person project meetings at any distant site, managers and team members alike will want pre-approval and buy-in from the powers that be.

One way companies try to keep costs down is to employ or hire as contractors people who live and work in areas where compensation is lower than at the main sites. Lower rates for work done in a distant location don't always translate to higher profits, however, and cost reduction should never be the driving factor behind a global development effort. As Fowler notes, "productivity differences between developers are far greater than salary differences."[15]

Differences in productivity levels cost dearly but so too does time have a cost. In an empirical study conducted by Herbsleb and Mockus, distributed software development is shown to take, on average, two-and-one-half times longer than collocated development.[16] The real incentives for running global projects include finding experts independent from headquarters or opening up new markets .

Communication Flow

My colleagues and I find it helpful to identify communication flow by tracing implicit social networks established in our projects. On global projects having dispersed and distributed teams, one viable alternative to observing people at one physical location is to track communication channels by means of online or written surveys to gather information, in effect, to visualize

---

[14]Pugh, op. cit., slide 59.

[15]See http://martinfowler.com/articles/agileOffshore.html updated (July 2006) at M. Fowler, "Using an Agile Software Process with Offshore Development," p. 12.

[16]D. Herbsleb and A. Mockus, "An Empirical Study of Speed and Communication in Globally Distributed Software Development," *IEEE Transactions on Software Engineering,* Vol. 29, No. 6 (June 2003), pp. 481-94.

interactions, as recommended in Scott .[17] I typically learn about my projects' social networks by means of a kind of human sociogram, conducted like so: During a team retrospective, I ask participants to position themselves close to people with whom they collaborate the most and away from those who interact the least.[18] I also ask participants to identify people with whom they collaborate *outside* their team structure, and then record the information on a white board or butcher's paper affixed to one wall of the room. Participants working, say, on a feature team could use this device to show interaction with other feature teams. People can also record communication channels and flow by drawing a picture or diagram to reflect interactions. Once a project's communication flow is thus analyzed, the knowledge can be used to improve the overall communication structure and as well as to strengthen collaboration at points where necessary.

4.3 Cultural Differences

All kinds of in-person and face-to-face meetings can help distributed teams cultivate understanding and mutual respect for others, but the experience of working at a different site is especially effective at instilling cultural awareness in team members. Such awareness is a necessity, in part because, as Lise Hvatum observes, "All cultures have their unwritten rules, and there are many examples of collaboration problems that stem from a lack of understanding of ethical and behavioral codes."[19]

The impact a different culture has on work is not always what it seems. For example, a company based in the United States was having difficulty understanding why development of its software in Russia was taking much longer than expected. Only after working for several iterations with the Russian team at its main site did the Americans understand that this team was set back

---

[17]J. Scott, *Social Network Analysis: A Handbook,* 2nd ed. (Thousand Oaks, Calif.: Sage, 1991).

[18]For more on retrospectives, see Chapter 8, "Eliciting Feedback and Conducting Retrospectives." See also N.L. Kerth, *Project Retrospectives: A Handbook for Team Reviews* (New York: Dorset House Publishing, 2001) for a comprehensive exploration.

[19]L.B. Hvatum, "Agile Practices and Distributed Teams," *Cutter IT Journal*, Vol. 20, No. 5 (May 2007), p. 7.

by frequent power outages, not by cultural differences. The Russian team was behind schedule because of infrastructure, not culture—a reason that only became clear when the Americans worked at the Russian site, giving each party the opportunity to learn from the other.[20] No matter what the reason is, you will most often gain an understanding only when you go there and learn from each other, which adheres to the lean principle of *genchi genbutsu*[21]. On-site exposure such as this is one of the reasons why the concept of expatriates are so important for dispersed teams.[22]

Most often, we assume that cultural differences only affect projects having people from different countries or speaking different languages working together. However, a colleague recently shared a story with me about cultural differences between a team in Minnesota collaborating with a team in Florida: During conference calls, one or two representatives from the northern site participated, taking in information to disseminate to the rest of the team after the call ended, whereas the entire southern team—close to twenty people—always participated in each call. My colleague's impression was that team members at the Florida site thought they would be excluded from future calls if they didn't participate in every one, thereby risking losing the respect of peers and counterparts. However, people at the Minnesota site seemed to have successfully established a culture of trust and communication, believing they would be fully informed by their peers. Without asking both teams for reasons, we cannot know what the real motivation was for these different behaviors, only that cultural differences can exist even where collaborators speak the same language and share the same shore. The challenge in such a scenario is that cultural differences can be subtle and hard to observe.

Learning to anticipate and address cultural differences can be challenging as well. For example, in some Asian cultures, team members will refrain from openly disagreeing, especially in conversation with a more-senior person. Moreover, if someone says, "Yes," he or she may only mean "Yes, I heard what you

---

[20]Thanks to David Hussman for sharing this experience (personal communication).

[21]Genchi genbutsu (Japanese) means "go and see for yourself", Jeffrey K. Liker. The Toyota Way. 14 Management Principles from the World's Greatest Manufacturer. McGraw-Hill. 2004, p. 233.

[22]I introduced the concept of expatriates in "Forging a Team" in chapter 3, "Building Teams".

said," and not necessarily, "Yes, I agree," or "Yes, I understand what you mean." To get to the bottom, my colleague Bas Vodde suggests always asking a question and then its opposite, because if someone responds yes to both questions, you will know you need to further clarify the meaning.[23] Further to his point, Bas told me about being in Japan and asking, "Is my English clear or do you need a translation?" The answer was yes, which made it clear the person didn't understand a word.

I'm not an ethnologist, so I won't go into detail about cultural tendencies. However, I do want to share some of my experiences that illustrate agile development challenges related to cultural differences.

Similarities versus Differences

Distance between people is characterized by geography, time, culture, language, politics, and history. Physical, or geographic, distance directly impacts communication. Allen maintains that if people are further apart than fifty meters, communication severely deteriorates.[24] The deterioration is in the same way severe whether physical distance between people correlates to their being located in different buildings, cities, countries, or continents.

Distance, as defined by physical proximity, will always influence the quality—the integrity—of relationships and communication. Carmel and Abbott suggest associating physical distance with difference and physical proximity with similarity: ". . . difference that imposes difficulties in the smooth operation of the sourcing relationship. Conversely, proximity, viewed here as the effect of reducing remoteness, is associated with *similarity*, similarity that enhances competitive advantage."[25] Thus, if people on a project focus on what they have in common with others, they can more easily bridge their differences. Sometimes, the culture of different sites can be rallied around similarities (for instance, around historical or linguistic origin). To create proximity within the project, a *project culture* must be developed, having to do,

---

[23] My thanks to Bas Vodde for this suggestion (personal communication).

[24] T. Allen, *Managing the Flow of Technology: Technology Transfer and the Dissemination of Technological Information Within the R&D Organization* (Cambridge, Mass.: MIT Press, 1984).

[25] E. Carmel and P. Abbott. "Why 'Nearshore' Means That Distance Matters," *Communications of the ACM*, Vol. 50, No. 10 (October 2007), pp. 42-43.

for example, with coding style or versioning or by emphasizing joint project history, typically at a retrospective.

Culture Fit

Cultural differences can be specific to particular companies. A company, no less than the broader society, can shape a culture that strongly influences its employees' behavior. Even a domain shapes a culture. Accountants, for example, typically work in a culture completely different from that of artists. Even if we stay within similar domains, and even within the same company, business analysts, say, are likely to have a culture slightly different from programmers, from testers, from managers. Different cultures can even exist inside a single domain, with the culture of a C++ programmer always different from that of a Smalltalk programmer[26]. These differences are even cultivated in the different domain-specific communities, making it likely that, say, programmers in the United States have more in common in terms of work style with programmers in India than with American business analysts.

Joint Project Culture

---

[26]Nowadays I should probably compare C++ programmers with Ruby programmers who both differ in culture as well.

Some cultures accommodate other cultures comparatively easily; many do not, but because most global projects take place in a predefined setting, choosing partners with whom to collaborate is not generally an option. Hofstede[27] has developed a model that quantifies behavioral differences in diverse cultures using an index. This model can be used for identifying which cultures fit best together or which sites can best collaborate both can help teams on global projects bridge the gaps between different cultures. Speaking to this point in an interview conducted by Philip Armour, Doug Grimsted, CEO of Aginity, explains his company's focus on matching cultures:

"We felt we had to have a culture that is closer to the U.S. We must have people who will tell us what we need to know, not what they think we want to hear."[28]

Crossing Big Boundaries by Ainsley Nies[a]

In 2002, I was asked to manage an international project with subteams in Asia, Europe, and North America, and no budget for travel. I knew that as a team we would face the typical communication problems with distributed international work, triggered by differences in time zone, language, and culture. As a project lead working from corporate headquarters, I also knew from experience that I could anticipate skepticism (a justifiably healthy dose) from the folks at non-corporate sites who become involved with corporate-led efforts.

Clearly all of these issues would be magnified without face-to-face contact—we needed a way to establish trust and lay the foundation for a collaborative work environment. We started by gathering feedback from the team about what had worked well, and not so well, for them in previous projects, and what the effects were. The information was synthesized and used to help design a project website (versus the more typical file-share type of solution at the time), and benefit began with the cross-team connections established during development. The site contained the expected project artifacts; however, it also had an entry

---

[27]Geert Hofstede and Gert Jan Hofstede. Cultures and Orgainzations: Software of the Mind. McGraw-Hill, 2nd edition. 2004

[28]P.G. Armour, "Agile . . . and Offshore: An Interview with a New Paradigm," *Communications of the ACM,* Vol. 50, No. 1 (January 2007), p. 14.

for each team member that included a photo, project role, work site location, local time, the weather report for that location, and optional personal information chosen by the team member (generally things like family, hobbies, pets, special interests, etc.).

This information enabled the team members to have a better sense of each other, open new lines of communication, develop richer relationships, and establish trust. There was also an important increased awareness of how what happens globally can affect each of us locally. People information *is* project information and requires (at least) equal emphasis for success.

[a]Ainsley Nies (USA). Project lead and facilitator.

Realistic Planning

Within a few iterations, agile-development team members learn their team velocity. This knowledge comes from estimating tasks at the beginning of an iteration, reflecting at the end of an iteration on achievements, and then planning approximately the same amount of work for the next iteration as the team delivered in the previous one. The process is called *Yesterday's Weather*, and it is based on the premise that a weather forecast is fairly likely to come true if you just predict that the weather tomorrow will be the same as it is today.[29] Yesterday's Weather protects individuals and teams from taking on too much work, supporting realistic planning and eliminating the probability of anyone needing to work overtime. As the Agile Manifesto states, "Agile processes promote sustainable development. The sponsors, developers, and users should be able to maintain a constant pace indefinitely."[30]

In most of my projects, it takes about five iterations for team velocity to stabilize. However, I have found that planning subsequent work based on the actual amount accomplished in the past

---

[29]Yesterday's Weather: http://c2.com/cgi/wiki?YesterdaysWeather. See also K. Beck and M. Fowler, *Planning Extreme Programming* (Reading, Mass.: Addison-Wesley, 2001).

[30]Agile Manifesto online: http://agilemanifesto.org/principles.html.

iteration seems to contradict with the culture of some teams. These teams tend to be overly ambitious and plan for too many tasks, although they know from past iterations that it won't be doable.

The way I deal with this problem is to double-check a team's past achievements and future estimates and then to encourage team members to reduce the scope to the same velocity exhibited in the past. Unfortunately, I usually find that I need to remind them for every iteration, making this more an exercise than a real solution, but it does convince some teams of the need for realistic planning.

Workload Responsibility

Agile approaches rely on self-organizing teams on which each team member assumes full responsibility for his or her share of the work and the team defines the work it will be responsible for accomplishing in the upcoming iteration.

That is the strategy, but most often, team members are not able to take up responsibility because neither they nor their managers, especially in large organizations, are used to this approach.[31] Instead, they're used to having management define the tasks and decide who will perform them and in what specific period of time. Inability to take responsibility is not solely the individual's dilemma; in fact, some companies discourage employees from taking responsibility. In some, just the size of the company could foster this behavior if people assume they will not be able to make any difference. In others, management doesn't recognize the power and asset of true leadership, and therefore people are used to command-and-control, which contradicts taking responsibility.

I have discovered that taking responsibility is most difficult for team members who work in a hierarchical culture. I have even encountered problems with taking responsibility in team members who indeed were raised with non-hierarchical family values, but whose parents were not and consequently were unable to submerse their children in the non-hierarchical culture! Such people very often are just used to command-and-control, not to taking responsibility for seeing tasks and ensuring that they get done.

---

[31] For more on shouldering responsibility, see Eckstein, op. cit., pp. 45-48.

Problem Reporting

At daily synchronization sessions, team members report problems they face, giving every team member the opportunity to gain the same understanding about the status of the project.[32] The practice is highly effective for small, collocated teams and projects, but it is less so when many people participate in the daily synchronization, particularly if participating over the phone or via some communications medium. Problems known to the report-giver may be glossed over or even omitted because he or she may just report quickly and fail to fully state the impediments. Problems also fail to get noted because a listener pays too little attention. Other possible reasons could be that the person reporting assumes that the problem is of no importance to the larger group, or wants to cover up the impediment, or doesn't want to prolong daily synchronization, and so on. Naturally you can experience such a behavior in an in-person meeting as well yet, a virtual meeting complicates uncovering it and amplifies the effect.

Detecting unstated problems is a challenge requiring people to listen carefully and interpret what is implicit in each report. Often, just one additional question will draw out the problem. Sometimes, however, following up with individuals separately after the daily synchronization will clarify how important knowledge of certain problems is to the whole group, and can reduce participants' fear that a problem report is perceived as a bad report.

Withholding or omitting information about problems affecting project status is bad practice, but the opposite behavior—seeing nothing except problems—is dangerous as well. Ultimately, it is up to the person leading the daily synchronization to keep problem statements on track.

Honest Feedback

Agility is fueled by frequent feedback, which can be given and obtained in various ways. For example, each team member can provide feedback during the daily synchronization; tests can provide feedback about the system; the delivered system is feedback on the project's progress; velocity provides feedback

---

[32] Daily synchronization is discussed in Chapter 9, "Customizing Practices."

about the advancement of the team toward the deadline. Feed-back provides information, but it is not always honest, objective information automatically reflecting reality.

To my dismay on one of my projects, team members faked the assertion statement of a test, missing the opportunity the feedback unit tests would provide.[33] When we dug deeper, we found that the problem was a team member's lack of skills, *not* a cultural difference or an attempt to deceive. This team member simply didn't yet know how to write proper tests.

On another project, there was one team that always provided positive feedback to peers about their velocity and their prob-ability of reaching deadlines. Only during individual conversa-tions and when working at their own site (when it was almost impossible to hide certain problems) were these team members able to provide honest feedback. I have seen this behavior often: Most of the time, you will receive honest feedback if you talk with people individually and in person.

The problem remains how to know whether it is necessary to talk with someone in person, one-to-one. There are definitely some obvious signs, like feedback that doesn't fit with your own perception, or feedback that seems static for a long time (no changes for better or for worse, which can't possibly be true). Consider whether the initially established relationship proved trusting, and continuously build and reinforce elements that promote forthright communication.

Noise

Although a lot of people bring up the topic of noise when describing first impressions about agile teams, the observation seems independent of whether or not the agile team is *global*. The major concern often voiced by people inexperienced with agile development is that agile teams are much noisier than other teams. This declaration is fueled by the reality that com-munication is taken seriously by agile teams, the whole team works together in the same room, and such practices as pair programming raise the noise level. Noise is rarely considered a problem by agile team members, as long as their work space is dedicated to people on the same project. If people from other

---

[33]A hint for budding unit-test detectives: Most of the tests ended with the statement xxx.assertTrue(true); .

projects share the same room, the agile team's conversation can be perceived as a disturbance.

However, noise can also be a cultural issue and is therefore specific to global development (and not to agile development). An Italian colleague shared with me his experiences in a global team with work sites in Italy and Japan. When team members worked together at a single location and also when they changed places, noise became a serious problem. The reason is that these cultures have a completely different understanding of noise. Whereas the Italians "talked loudly almost all the time" (as my Italian colleague put it), the Japanese most often worked silently. When talking, Japanese team members used quiet voices, which led to Italian team members not listening to them because they couldn't really hear what was being said.

Cultural challenges such as noisy conversation most often can be easily resolved once people are made aware something's an issue, only needing to be reminded from time to time to take different cultures into consideration.

Humor

Humor, irony, and sarcasm do not easily translate between languages, cultures, and backgrounds. Using them can cause offense if misunderstood. A colleague reports that on a project distributed between the United Kingdom and the United States, the irony of British team members was completely misinterpreted by the Americans to mean exactly the opposite of what the Brits intended.[34] Even if you think you speak the same language, culture imprints humor as well. As Pugh succinctly sums it up, "Humor doesn't export (or import)."[35]

Communication Media

Frequent communication not only keeps a project alive, it is essential to detecting and solving problems. However, distributed team communication can be difficult, compounded by people with different mother tongues trying to understand each other in a second or third language. For introverts, talking out loud is already difficult. To do so in a second language is particularly

---

[34] L.B. Hvatum, personal communication.

[35] Pugh, op. cit., slide 71.

intimidating if other people are more adept in that language. In order to discover each team member's competence and comfort levels, use various modes of communication that address different persons differently, respecting their unique sensory modalities.[36]

Pay attention to the ways your team communicates and ensure that important information is communicated in multiple ways. Yes, this recommendation advocates redundancy, but if the benefit is that every team member is on the same page, it is worthwhile.

Choices in Communication Media

Furthermore, be sensitive to communication media that don't work in all contexts or for all people. For example, some people consider e-mail to be offensive, annoying, and inappropriately informal, preferring to communicate by telephone exchange or face-to-face[37]. Other people may prefer communicating by e-mail and other forms of written correspondence because these allow them to take time formulating what they want to say or use a dictionary to clarify what has been communicated—tasks

---

[36] For more on sensory modalities, see Eckstein, op. cit., pp. 61-62.

[37] I discuss "Tools" for communication in detail in chapter 5 "Keeping Sites in Touch"

that are made more difficult with synchronous conversations. It is especially important for globally dispersed and distributed teams to evaluate different communication media and regularly check what supports and what hinders communication within and across teams and make adjustments accordingly. Karolak puts the emphasis thusly:

"On-the-fly adjustments are an important part of communications in a virtual team. You may use e-mail one day, a fax the next, and real-time telephoning the next. Team members need to be made aware of each other's needs and to have communications resources they can configure as needed."[38]

4.4 Summary

"Trust needs touch;"[39] it is therefore very important to help team members get to know each other and the different project sites. Proximity among team members can be created by conducting regular joint meetings, exchanging people between sites, and meeting longer and more frequently at the beginning of a project. Keep in mind the limitations of reconciling cultures, as Krishna, Sahay, and Walsham point out:

"Major differences in norms and values cannot be harmonized, since they derive from deep-seated differences in cultural background, education, and working life. Examples include attitudes toward hierarchy and power and different business practices."[40]

Moreover, be aware of the communication and trust threshold, to avoid breaching it by ignoring the necessity of proximity. Tools and technology can help preserve relationships and collaboration on work, but they do not eliminate the need for face-to-face contact yet, as Dale Karolak points out:

"The more virtual the organization, the more people need to meet in person. This does not mean daily, of course, but there should be some plan to have the team members meet regularly,

---

[38] D.W. Karolak, *Global Software Development: Managing Virtual Teams and Environments* (Los Alamitos, Calif.: IEEE Computer Society Press, 1998), p. 70.

[39] Handy, op. cit., pp. 40-50.

[40] S. Krishna, S. Sahay, and G. Walsham, "Managing Cross-Cultural Issues in Global Software Outsourcing," *Communications of the ACM*, Vol. 47, No. 4 (April 2004), p. 65.

say, every other month or at least quarterly in a year-long project." [41]

The reason is, that this threshold will be reached after eight to twelve weeks of relying on electronic communication only.

Another very important means for creating trust and mutual respect is acknowledging the different sites by holding the diverse in-person meetings alternately at the various sites. This way everyone will not only get an idea what it is like working at this site, but as well having the pleasure of being the host or the guest variantly.

Finally, you have to acknowledge the different cultures involved in the project team. These can influence agile development as well. For example the different attitudes in taking responsibility can have a great impact on your development process in place.

---

[41] D.W. Karolak, *Global Software Development: Managing Virtual Teams and Environments* (Los Alamitos, Calif.: IEEE Computer Society Press, 1998), p. 19.

5. Keeping Sites in Touch

We agree only with one another
if we sense some commonality amongst ourselves.

— Jean de la Bruyère

The greater the physical distance between sites and the more sites involved on a project, the more difficult and expensive it is to keep the sites connected and the less likely it is that the project can succeed. Some experts recommend that distributed projects never spread over more than three sites, maintaining that anything larger will be almost impossible to synchronize, and Carmel and Tjia advocate, "Reduce the number of project locations as much as possible."[1]

For building trust, creating mutual understanding and respect it is important to bring the team members together. Therefore, I want to bring –again– the following principle to your attention "the most efficient and effective method of conveying information to and within a development team is face-to-face conversation."[2]

Carmel and Tjia also encourage that communication between locations be conducted in different ways and on different levels, advising against having a single point of contact for each site, a practice that ". . . does not necessarily contribute to effective governance. Effective offshore governance requires multiple channels of communication at different levels and different locations."[3]

To stay properly connected and to ensure that the communication and trust threshold will not be breached, teams at

---

[1] E. Carmel and P. Tjia, *Offshoring Information Technology: Sourcing and Outsourcing to a Global Workforce* (Cambridge, Eng.: Cambridge University Press, 2005), p. 172.

[2] Agile principles: http://agilemanifesto.org/principles.html

[3] Ibid., op. cit., p. 144.

distributed project sites may make use of communication facilitators, ambassadors, social connections, and tools, as the following sections will explore.

5.1 Communication Facilitator

A communication facilitator helps to ensure trust between sites and "is responsible for visiting all the teams regularly, obtaining feedback, and discovering deficiencies and (potential) problems, possibly solving them immediately."[4] If the project is extremely large and heavily distributed, more than one communication facilitator may be needed.

Please note that I'm talking about a role here. On some of my projects, we defined this role as a full-time position; on others, we asked team members in different positions to additionally fulfill the role. Often, people who already are working with project members from different sites (the chief architect, for example) will take on the role of communication facilitator. Whoever takes on the task, however, must be someone who is socially qualified, who people unequivocally will respect and trust.

Ambler suggests supporting the connection between different sites with a traveler "who works at one site for a few days or weeks, then moves to another site to work there for some time. Travelers help to share information among team members and keep everyone in sync both culturally and technically."[5]

Communication Facilitator as Ombudsman

I've found that it's best that the communication facilitator is not a manager, or at least not someone imbued with specific authority and, therefore, can fulfil this role more as an ombudsman than as a controller.

Team members are most likely to respect and trust a communication facilitator who truly is an ombudsman to whom existing problems can be reported and who will investigate them, report findings, provide solutions, and help to achieve equitable settlements.

---

[4]J. Eckstein, op. cit., p. 67.

[5]S. Ambler, op. cit.

Technical and Social Prowess

Most often, team members talk to communication facilitators about technical problems, making a facilitator's technical knowledge very important. However, it's seldom that *real* technical issues are raised, rather that team members talk about social or communication problems masquerading as technical problems. The communication facilitator must not only be technically skilled but also socially skilled in order to unmask these technical issues to address the causes behind the symptoms. Otherwise, team members may quickly decide that the communication facilitator won't understand their needs. The communication facilitator must prove that it is useful to discuss issues with her or him by providing support reflecting team members' requests. Facilitators must educate team members about how their concerns relate to underlying problems, or team members may regard assistance as flogging a dead horse.

Management By Flying Around

An effective management style is the so-called management by walking around (MBWA). MBWA focuses on personal contact between management and workers. The idea is based on the fact that a person can learn much more in a face-to-face conversation than from indirect contact. Managers overhear what goes on and get a feeling for the real status of a project.

In a distributed team, this isn't doable by walking around. Instead, management and all other key persons, such as the communication facilitator, the chief architect, and the product owner, have to fly around. As Carmel notes, "The global software manager practices Management By Flying Around (MBFA). He makes sure to have face-to-face time with team members at all sites."[6] Only MBFA will ensure that all teams share the same vision and that key people are aware of the problems the different teams face. Carmel stresses furthermore that there is no alternative to MBFA, "Conversely, too many virtual managers resort to management by e-mailing around. . . . Asking a remote team to get a task done by a certain deadline is not nearly as effective as flying there to make sure that they get it done on time."[7]

---

[6]E. Carmel, op. cit., p. 189.

[7]E. Carmel and P. Tjia, op. cit., p. 170.

Thus, for every manager of a distributed project travelling or flying frequently is a must.

5.2 Ambassador

Finally, there is something we can learn from politics. When one nation wants to foster a relationship with another nation, it opens an embassy in the other nation. The ambassador is then the direct connection to this other nation, most often just by being present, "overhearing" what's going on, and reporting back to his or her home country. The ambassador also represents the home country and delivers information from that to the host nation. By being both a listener and a spokesperson, the ambassador is the home country's representative and has primary responsibility for ensuring the communication flow between different sites.

Ambassador

Site Representation

Exactly the same job the politically appointed ambassador fulfills is required in a distributed project. Each site needs a representative at the other site(s).[8] Distinct from feature-team representatives, site representatives might represent several teams and team members located at the ambassador's home location. Representing the home site means mainly to establish what my colleague David Hussman calls a *cross-shore communication,* ensuring communication between different sites in both directions.[9]

In most projects, the concept of ambassadors is implemented unidirectional. Either ambassadors represent the main site at remote locations or only one ambassador for each site is present at the main site. For explaining the latter as an example, if Germany is the main site and Russia and Ireland are distant sites, most typically there will be one Russian and one Irish representative in Germany and neither a Russian ambassador in Ireland nor a German ambassador in Russia. The primary reason for this is that most distributed teams are centrally coordinated.

So long as the development effort is centrally coordinated, it usually will be adequate to have ambassadors at the main site representing distributed sites.[10] From the main site, representatives will keep abreast of project status by flying to and from the distant sites. But if the development effort is globally integrated, or rather in or about to enter the third stage of Carmel's three-stage evolution of global development, it is absolutely necessary that every site has an ambassador at each site. Otherwise, coordination among distributed sites will falter.

Characteristics and Competency

Not every team member is qualified to be an ambassador and, furthermore, not every team member will want to make the sacrifices associated with being far from home for a (longer) period of time. People selected to serve as ambassadors must be able to maintain contact with the home site and be courageous

---

[8] M. Fowler, loc. cit.

[9] D. Hussman, "Offshore Agile Software Development" *Proceedings of XP 2005* (Sheffield, Eng., 2005).

[10] See Chapter 2, "Assessing Agility for Global Projects," for more on centrally coordinated efforts.

enough to state and represent that site's position without getting into trouble at the embassy site. In addition, ambassadors must be well respected and possess soft skills that allow them to understand and translate all concerns from one site to another.

Determining which potential ambassadors are willing to travel is important to project success. There are always some people who like to travel; others are okay with it as long as it won't be forever; and some don't like it at all, or cannot commit to it for personal reasons, or even completely fear traveling.

To prevent having one person off-site for the whole project, generate a pool of ambassadors. Even people who like to travel may not wish to move somewhere for several years. One of the problems is that these people will lose their social connections at home. Furthermore, if an ambassador stays at the embassy site for the whole project, it is very likely that he or she will lose touch with good contacts at the home site. Thus, after a while people get too adjusted and can therefore not represent their site anymore. On one of my projects, we experienced this problem when a customer stayed on-site for the duration of the project. That customer enjoyed working with us so much that she stopped identifying with the other customers, and identified instead with us. Consequently, she couldn't provide the valuable feedback we had hoped to gain.

Travel Schedule

Once a pool of ambassadors has been selected, determine how the ambassadors should take turns. Iterations provide a good basis for scheduling, with, say, ambassadors exchanged at the end of every iteration. A different scheduling could be devised depending on how far embassies are from the home site, how difficult travel to specific embassies will be, and so on.

Avoid having the same people taking the role of the ambassador for the project's lifetime. Instead ensure a regular exchange of the ambassadors.

It is helpful to make ambassadors' schedules at each site public so everyone knows who is the ambassador at which site during which iteration. The project's wiki is a good place to post this schedule. Also make public the contact information for all ambassadors, especially phone numbers and e-mail addresses that differ from their home site's contact information.

Concrete Tasks

In addition to representing their home site, ambassadors have responsibility for taking part in the daily Scrum of Scrums.[11] If there are different levels of Scrum of Scrums—for example, a regularly scheduled Site-Scrum of Scrums at the home site as well as at the embassy site—ambassadors need to attend both[12]. Ambassadors who have an additional role, for example, as a regular member of a feature team, will also attend the feature team's daily synchronization. Yes, this often means that an ambassador will be on the phone at irregular hours, but careful scheduling may ease the burden.

All impediments that come up during the Scrum of Scrums and the daily synchronization that are related to communication and coordination between the home site and the embassy site are action items the ambassador will need to address, such as the following:

- ensuring that people answer phones and e-mails across sites
- gathering the right people to solve problems
- transferring required knowledge

Fowler notes an additional area for which ambassadors must be responsible: "An important part of the ambassador's job is to communicate gossip. On any project, there's a lot of informal communication. While much of this isn't important, some of it is—and the trouble is that you can't tell which is which."[13]

5.3 Social Connections

Another important element in the quest to establish mutual respect and trust between locations centers on how well social

---

[11] See Chapter 9, "Practices," for more information on Scrum of Scrums.

[12] Site-Scrum of Scrums is a (daily) synchronization across all subteams residing at the same site. More details on Site-Scrum of Scrums in Chapter 9, "Practices".

[13] M. Fowler, loc. cit.

connections between sites are nurtured. Social events additionally enforce the focus on cultural similarities rather than differences[14].

Joint Celebration

Whenever the overall project reaches a goal, the dispersed and distributed teams responsible for the success should celebrate their achievement jointly. This joint celebration increases pride in work and fosters a culture of achievement. Getting the whole gang together at one location may not always be feasible, but an alternative is to hold celebrations at different sites with, say, a web cam connection among sites. Recordings and pictures allow sharing the celebrations at the different sites despite great differences in time zones. Additionally, joint celebrations reduce the danger that teams will breach the trust and communication threshold as project members share a positive experience and the benefits of staying in touch.

Picture Power

Whether people see each other often or not, enhance their connectedness with pictures. We typically post photographs of each team member together with contact information on the project wiki and encourage feature teams to provide pictures of each iteration's review and planning meeting.[15] Photos help people catch up with each other after time apart, and even provide value after someone spends time away from the site for a vacation or an illness. Moreover, pictures provide a nice way for newbies on the project to learn names and faces.

Everyday Life

A colleague reports that having a web cam installed at each site, say, near the coffee machine or water cooler helps people at connected sites feel close-knit and serves to preserve trust between sites. Other members of distributed projects meet

---

[14]For more on focusing on "Similarities versus Differences", see Chapter 4, "Establishing Communication and Trust."

[15]For more on meeting planning, see Chapter 7, "Ensuring Business Value." For review-meeting planning, see Chapter 8, "Eliciting Feedback and Conducting Retrospectives."

irregularly in a virtual café to discuss whatever topics come up. Discussion may be work related, but most often is not, for example, with many people taking advantage of the opportunity to discuss the latest games of the soccer World Cup.

Travel Tips

My projects always post travel information on our wiki. Typically, we include information about which airline provides the best connections and whether travel to the site from airports, bus, or train stations is best done by rental car, taxi, or public transportation. We also provide tips about what costs to expect and which credit cards are accepted. Probably the most important information we collect pertains to local attractions and activities, identifying recommended restaurants and pubs as well as sightseeing trips. Travel tips can make traveling easier—it is often enough a hassle—and more fun.

Enjoyable Travel

5.4 Tools

When people are not able to get together in person, tools as commonplace as, say, a telephone for calling somebody or a computer or PDA with e-mail capability can make needed communication and collaboration more feasible. Finding the right tools to assist people in accomplishing tasks associated with distributed projects is important, making it essential that team members identify specific requirements before choosing tools. For example, such factors as the number of people who must be contacted, required speed or accuracy, and whether information will be dispensed in output mode only or collaboratively exchanged all influence the selection process and are examined in the following:

- *Number of people:* Sometimes, only one person needs to be contacted; at other times, a whole group must be reached. The best tool to use depends on the number of people and whether it matters if information communicated one-on-one might be transmitted to the rest of a group or not.

- *Response time:* Now and then, instant feedback is needed; at other times, feedback can come with a slight delay; sometimes, even a long delay is acceptable. The best tool to use depends on whether a person wants only to make peers aware of something, which doesn't require instant feedback, or urgently seeks salient advice and responses.
- *Unidirectional or multi-directional:* Sometimes, a piece of work or a project artifact must be shown to one colleague; sometimes, it must be shown to a group of people, all of whom need to see the same picture; and sometimes, just showing something is not enough because people must work on a task together, albeit remotely. The best tool to use depends on whether collaborative interaction among team members is required or whether information flow is enough.

Identifying the reasons behind the virtual contact among remote sites, allows you to select the most appropriate tools for communication. You have to acknowledge that these tools can only support but never substitute healthy collaboration and communication .

Direct Connections

To facilitate communication, I highly recommend that teams compile and make available to all project members a central directory of members' names, job locations, phone numbers (cellular, fax, and land lines), e-mail addresses, and other relevant accounts (instant messaging, for example). Avoid listing indirect contact information, such as phone numbers or e-mail addresses that first connect to a secretary's office, and appoint someone at each site to be responsible for keeping that site's data up-to-date. Posting the directory on the project's internal wiki conveys the importance to all team members of keeping posted, personal information confidential while allowing everyone quick access and eliminating time wasted searching for current contact information. An additional benefit from publishing direct contact information for *all* members is that it seeds trust, showing that everyone relies on everyone else to keep the information confidential and not to abuse those connection points.

Synchroneity versus Asynchroneity

Synchronous conversations allow team members to communicate simultaneously. For example, if I meet my friend in the street and we start talking, we are both in a conversation at the same time. Asynchronous communication involves people "speaking" with each other at different times. For instance, if I leave a note for my family on the kitchen table before I leave the house, my family can read it and respond back with another note whenever time permits.

Although synchronous tools are often experienced as being richer, more efficient forms of communication, they are also more difficult to use than asynchronous tools. The richness comes from the immediacy of the communication and feedback. The difficulty is that synchronous tools do not allot much time for participants to digest what they hear and respond adequately. Synchronous communication may be especially difficult for shy or introverted people, and even more so for people who lack confidence about their language skills, especially if they are asked to use their second or third language.

Asynchronous tools have the big advantage not to interrupt the actual work and allowing participants to take as much time (well, within reason) as they need to understand what's being proposed or requested. Tools such as e-mail and fax allow participants time to construct a reply, consult their peers and a dictionary, and feel confident about their response (and about the question). A great disadvantage of many asynchronous tools is lack of proximity and instantaneousness between communicators, possibly putting trust between parties in jeopardy because most often neither party can see or hear its counterpart and cannot be sure of the intended meaning. The missing direct feedback leads often to missing each other's point. Non-literal linguistic characteristics (like irony) are even more difficult for recipients to comprehend when written than spoken.

As there are pros and cons for both synchronous and asynchronous communication, the important thing is for project members to use all kinds of communication channels to enrich the exchange of information, and to allow all kinds of people to identify their preferred way to communicate with their peers.

Audio and Video

Videoconferencing generally is perceived as a powerful communication medium, but for the daily synchronization my projects have not experienced it to be more powerful than audio tools (telephone and conference calls). For meetings where we need to display or point to something, videoconferencing help us a great deal. Research by Bekkering and Shim finds that "the visual image does not contribute much more information than what audio alone can provide. This finding is consistent with previous studies of lie detection in videoconferencing. . . . Of course, video can assist communication in ways other than improving trust or detecting lies, for example, by allowing participants to demonstrate an action or object."[16] Another application of video is knowledge transfer. Tutorials and presentations can be recorded and project members can watch them whenever time permits. Bekkering and Shim's research concludes as well that trust perception is higher with both audio- and videoconferencing than with e-mail.

For daily synchronization meetings, the telephone is not only a great tool; it also is preferable to e-mail to clarify misunderstandings. The phone is a helpful tool as well for maintaining communication and trust because it allows synchronous and direct connection. However, phone usage has drawbacks such as the following:

- *Response pressure:* As with all synchronous communication tools, telephone communication requires participants to respond immediately in some fashion or other—it does not necessarily require answers or final decisions, of course, just acknowledgment that information has been exchanged. Immediate substantive response is sometimes difficult, especially if language is an obstacle or people don't feel comfortable voicing ideas. Especially when using the phone, team members should take care to speak slowly and clearly and use simple vocabulary.

---

[16]E. Bekkering and J.P. Shim, "Trust in Videoconferencing," *Communications of the ACM*, Vol. 49, No. 7 (July 2006), p. 106.

- *Line quality:* Inferior phone-line quality can lead to misunderstandings and, in turn, disturb trustful relationships. Static, dropped connections, and technological interruptions shouldn't be much of an issue anymore, but still can be at some places in the world.
- *Interruptions:* A phone call means always an instant interrupt of the actual work. If this turns into a problem, you should consider defining explicit phone times (or quiet times).

Instant Messaging

Many distributed teams use instant messaging (IM) to talk to team members at different locations. Instant messaging preserves a direct connection, which supports and builds trust, but cannot compensate for all the conversation required for a healthy project. Very often, IM is used as a steppingstone to a different communication channel (for example, people start talking via messaging to agree on a good time for a phone call).

Benefits of instant messaging include the following:

- *Accessibility:* Instant messaging tools enable communicators to know who is online and immediately reachable, eliminating guesswork about how long it will take to get a reply. In contrast to e-mail, when it sometimes feels as if all correspondence ends up in a black hole, instant messaging is transmitted when the receiver is online.
- *Timely feedback:* Because people necessarily are online when using their instant messaging tool, they are able to respond quickly, if not completely.

The instantaneousness of IM is also one of its most serious drawbacks—it interrupts people at all times. Consider defining specific times when people will be reachable and times they shouldn't be interrupted. Often, it is safeguard enough if people are aware that it is okay to shut down instant messaging from time to time.

Instant messaging facilitates synchronous conversation in the sense that a person cannot start a conversation unless a counterpart is simultaneously available, but IM communicators can delay conversation for an instant to rethink an answer or to check a reference.

E-mail

E-mail shares the advantages of all asynchronous tools (and, of course, as well their disadvantages). The biggest advantage is that respondents can take as much time as needed to answer e-mail. Of course, the argument can be made that this advantage is true for face-to-face conversation and instant messaging as well, but normally such behavior is much more widely accepted with e-mail.

The greatest disadvantage of e-mail is that it makes it too easy for a person to "talk" without "listening," sending information less as a dialogue and more as a one-way, outward flow of commentary. Such e-mail abuse might start with someone's idea of setting up a distribution list for the whole project so everyone "overhears" all ongoing conversation, a practice that leads, say, to team members in the United States receiving e-mails in which colleagues in Ireland invite each other to share cookies in the kitchen. Despite their occasional irrelevance, this kind of e-mail can be useful because, as Bas Vodde notes, "it creates a better understanding between the different sites. . . . I might ask someone at another site how the cookies are. This kind of informal conversation helps build trust."[17]

Informal information can bring out interesting facts, like the birthday of a colleague. However, such e-mail is more often annoying because it just fills inboxes, burying more important messages, desensitizing recipients to valuable conversation, and might cause people to stop reading e-mails altogether. On my distributed projects, therefore, I recommend that all distribution lists be carefully defined and used purposefully.

Another problem is the long e-mail chain, which is created by often-wonderful and important discussions between people on a team or in some special-interest group. As discussion goes on, people add their opinions in e-mail they insert in front of all other e-mails or embed in another's message, and then forward the chain, unmindful that important facts and decisions are buried in a long e-mail. Moving such discussions from e-mail to a wiki collaboration platform rescues the information from being transient (in e-mail) to persistent (on the platform), making it available to all project members, whether or not they take part in the discussion. An additional benefit is that topics posted on

---

[17]B. Vodde, personal communication.

a collaboration platform are searchable, versioned, and can be structured in a meaningful way.

Virtual Space

Some projects use chat rooms or facilities such as SecondLife to meet virtually, primarily to develop or maintain social connections.[18] I do know, however, of one project that successfully uses SecondLife for its dispersed daily synchronization and for remote pair programming[19].

Common Repository

Collocated and distributed projects alike benefit from an access point at which every project document can be found, allowing shared access to all documents as well as versioning for all code and tests—in fact, for every document of the project as for instance the project plan or the ambassadors' schedule etc. On my projects, we accomplish shared access by storing all kinds of files in a configuration and version management tool, accessible to and from all locations via intra- or Internet. Please ensure that the established security concept allows every project member at every location the access to the common repository[20]. We store information that is not file-based on our major collaboration platform wiki. Different brands of wikis all seem to provide for versioning and thus allow people to access earlier versions of stored information.

Wiki and other Collaboration Platforms

Very often, a global project's teams need to look at the same artifacts simultaneously. For instance, in a dispersed daily synchronization, every member of the feature team will want to see the iteration plan. At another time, one team member will want to explain a feature or process to the rest of the team. Happily, a number of tools support dispersed collaboration (eRoom, SharePoint, and NetMeeting, for example).

---

[18]For more on SecondLife, see http://www.secondlife.com.

[19]More on dispersed daily synchronizations and on remote pair programming in Chapter 9, "Customizing Practices".

[20]More on security in Chapter 6, "Ensuring Development and Delivery".

Time and again, it is not enough for members of a distributed group merely to see the same artifact, but instead must work concurrently on an artifact without being at the same location. For example, if a dispersed feature team wants to create a design jointly for a feature, every feature-team member needs to be able to actually change the design. A wiki can make a simple tool that dispersed and distributed team members can use for working together remotely—but, although most wikis successfully support collaboration on written artifacts, they fall short on graphic ones. More usually, collaboration tools support transferring control over changes to an artifact to a specific person in a virtual meeting allowing everyone only in turns to make changes. This virtual collaboration is not the same as a collaboration in which people working jointly on the same artifact stand as a group around a flipchart or whiteboard and develop a design. Therefore, you might consider looking into virtual or shared whiteboards which resemble this way of working for distributed teams[21].

From time to time, you have to rethink the structure of the wiki and make according adjustments so that the wiki stays helpful for the project also in the long run. Ignoring this provides the risk that although all information is stored in the wiki, you won't be able to find anything due to its complexity.

Typically, collaboration tools enrich communication across a distance and work best when additionally supported by audio tools. Using a tool like wiki while connected by phone or video makes perfect sense if people want to discuss changes while showing the topic at hand.

5.5 Summary

Koh, et al., identify four stimulation drivers that enable successful virtual communities as *leader involvement, off-line interaction, usefulness,* and *infrastructure quality.*[22] Leader involvement is critical for building relationships and is one reason why the leaders in distributed projects need to implement the strategy of Management By Flying Around so they can ensure the relationships between all sites. Off-line interaction increases

---

[21]An example of such a shared whiteboard is: AgilePlanner: http://ase.cpsc.ucalgary.ca/ase/index.php/AgilePlanning/Home/

[22]B.J. Koh, et al., op. cit., p. 71.

social presence. If people are working off-line together and have to build awareness of their peers through off-line interactions, they can do so through joint celebrations. Off-line interactions help team members understand, trust, and identify with one another, providing a stronger base for online community activity.

If team members can equate interacting seamlessly with usefulness, they most likely will contribute successfully to achieving team goals. Many teams need to remind themselves to stick to the rules for daily synchronization or for the Scrum of Scrums because these teams discovered that breaking these rules made these meetings only productive for and relevant to a few, but not all, participants. Following the rules rigorously can ensure that all team members participate and share relevant materials. So whenever you are asking people to collaborate you need to ensure the individual usefulness of the collaboration.

Infrastructure quality typically is essential to successful collaboration between and among team members. A great phone connection, easy access to the project wiki, and the trust and respect of teammates signal a viable distributed project infrastructure. In addition, as Koh, et al., observe, "in any virtual community, satisfactory system response time is generally viewed as a necessary requirement."[23]

For keeping the different sites in touch you will mainly need direct connections through people who are taking care to establish and preserve those. Although the ambassador has the strongest role in fulfilling this task, other people, like the managers will have to work on this as well. Keeping the different sites in touch requires time for informal communication, Daniela Damian reported[24]:

"Lack of informal communication in global teams negatively impacts relationship building [...]"

Special events, like celebrating a release together and technology, like sharing pictures on the project wiki will help as well to create a closer connection than the one that physically exists. However, even good collaboration tools won't help solving all collaboration problems. The precondition is establishing a good

---

[23] Ibid.

[24] Daniela Damian. Stakeholders in Global Requirements Engineering: Lessons Learned from Practice. In IEEE Software, March / April 2007. Page 21-27 (quoted from p. 24)

and working collaboration first, before supporting this collaboration by adequate tools. When selecting a tool, you have to be aware that most of the tools follow and support a specific management strategy, for instance command and control, or at the other end – trusted leadership.

However, nothing works better for establishing and preserving a trustful connection than actually meeting in person. Therefore, you need to find ways allowing project members to meet from time to time.

6. Ensuring Development and Delivery

People love chopping wood.
In this activity one immediately sees results.

— Albert Einstein

The third principle of the Agile Manifesto mandates, "Deliver working software frequently, from a couple of weeks to a couple of months, with a preference to the shorter timescale."[1] In order to frequently deliver working software that gives value to customers by meeting their feature requests and change requirements, software developers must address many challenges associated with distributed projects. The methods used to develop such software need to be driven by observation and experience and supported by an empirical process. As Ken Schwaber co-creator of Scrum notesnotes, "With an empirical process, you have a whole different control mechanism. . . . you have to monitor constantly in order to make adjustments."[2]

In this chapter, I focus on aspects of delivery, and not so much on the value of the software.[3] Delivery in a *release*—that is, a grouping of a series of iterations that provides meaningful functionality for the customer—can require extra planning but will not necessarily require extra work because the release just groups whatever functionality is accomplished by the release date together with the most recent iteration belonging to the same release. However, depending on the complexity of the project, the requirements regarding delivery, and the like, a team may decide to conduct a special iteration—called a *release iteration* or *stabilization iteration*—that will result in delivery

---

[1] Agile Manifesto online: http://agilemanifesto.org/principles.html.

[2] K. Schwaber, as quoted in J.A. Highsmith, *Agile Software Development Ecosystems* (Reading, Mass.: Addison-Wesley, 2002), p. 108.

[3] Delivering Value is the focus of Chapter 7, "Ensuring Business Value."

of a shippable product. The focus of a release iteration is not to develop new functionality but instead to hone existing functionality already developed in previous iterations into a shippable product.

6.1 Iterations

Agile teams allocate to shorter development cycles work that can be done by diverse feature teams in a relatively short timeframe, thereby enabling the development team to give customers value at most cycles' end. Shorter development cycles help feature teams to organize work, but also to deliver parts of a product.

Iteration Length

In both global and local agile development, two-week-long iterations provide organizations with a good way to deal with the uncertainty about the customers' needs and getting feedback on the true status of a project, assuming, of course, that the diverse feature teams do in fact deliver at the end of the time allocated for the iteration.

How long an iteration should last depends on a multitude of factors, such as balancing risk reduction by obtaining frequent feedback and accomplishing something meaningful in the available timeframe. Projects planning long iterations sometimes schedule a sanity check in the middle of the iteration to check on status and to verify whether development is proceeding as planned or falling behind. In my view, any iteration that calls for a sanity check (also called a *mid-sprint review)* is a smell[4] that signals that the iteration length most likely is too long. The wish for such mid-iteration checks is that people are not sure about the status of the project, because the last time they obtained feedback was too long ago. Instead of scheduling a mid-iteration check, consider shortening the iteration length and get to the bottom of the problem rather than treating its symptoms.

Every so often, people ask me whether the length of an iteration must be prolonged in a distributed setting because of the higher coordination effort required between sites. My response is that

---

[4]A smell is a hint to a problem.

iteration planning works the other way around: Because of the increased risk when developing globally, projects should reduce the length of development cycles in order to obtain feedback more frequently. This strategy buys a team time to act instead of leaving it time only to react after the fact. Indeed, the majority of distributed projects tend to shorten development cycles to reduce risk.[5] If you follow this majority, then you have the advantage to steer correctively based on status information contained in more frequently received feedback.

Done-Done

Agile practitioners term features as being in a *done-done* state to communicate readiness for delivery.[6] We use the term to avoid confusion and to eliminate ambiguity. I have often heard feature-team members proclaim that a feature is done, but when it comes to presenting the system, the feature doesn't work. My answer (at that time as a programmer) was always „I don't know, it worked before". The main problem is that what people mean by "done" might be any one of the following states:

- The feature has been developed.
- The feature has been tested.
- The feature has been integrated.
- The feature works in the test or production environment.
- The feature is ready to deliver to the customer.
- The feature is in production.

Very often, people have only the first few meanings in mind when they state that a feature is done. Done-done, however, refers to a feature that has arrived at the last state—that is, the feature has been developed, tested, integrated, documented, and works as desired in the production environment—and could (theoretically or actually) be delivered to the customer and go into production. Only this state of a feature provides people with accurate feedback on the actual status of the project, and, only features that are done-done factor into calculating feature-team velocity at the end of an iteration.[7]

---

[5] M. Fowler, loc. cit.

[6] I heard this term used the first time by Mary Poppendieck, author of Lean Software Development.

[7] I discuss team velocity in detail in Chapter 7, "Ensuring Business Value."

In fact, it will be nigh impossible for a distributed project to deliver a system unless all project teams agree on the definition that marks the completion of a feature.

Project Heartbeat

I regard iterations as the heartbeat of a project. When in sync across all sites, iterations constitute a continuous rhythm that allows teams to plan, do, inspect, and then adapt based on current feedback. Iterations keep a system alive, and serve as measurable indicators of the health of the whole system. Ideally, the whole system has the same rhythm, with iterations synchronized across all sites and across all feature teams.

At times, differences may disrupt the rhythm. For example, distributed teams may have members in different countries or with different religious beliefs who are absent on different holidays, which may slow a team so that it is out of sync with others. But you need to ensure that such differences do not break the rhythm completely. Because if your project is using different rhythms (that is different iteration lengths), you can regard this as a sign that individuals or individual teams focus on individual goals and not on the overall goal of the project.

Delivery Delay

As has been noted, a goal of agile methods is to deliver a version of the working product at the end of every iteration, but problems such as the following can inhibit or prevent delivery of every planned feature in the done-done state:

- *Delayed hardware:* On a project concurrently developing, say, an embedded application as well as the requisite hardware, hardware development is unlikely to keep pace with feature development. One strategy is to deliver new features on an older version of the hardware—assuming the version does support the required interfaces. Alternatively, another strategy is to approve features on a simulator. However, both of these strategies produce features that are not done-done, making it necessary to plan done-done delivery later on when the hardware is available to finally deploy those features.

- *Extensive testing:* Sometimes, a feature may be developed, tested, and integrated within one iteration, but overall system testing cannot be performed within the timeframe of the same iteration. Most often, this problem occurs if system tests are done manually and therefore require too much time to perform, and system test is therefore delayed until tests can be gradually automated. On other occasions, extensive load and performance tests might be needed, or the system is for other reasons too big to test within the same iteration as feature development. Larman notes testing delay is particularly problematic for projects with several teams.[8] In such cases, test pipelining executes tests one iteration later than the iteration in which the feature is developed, delaying done-done feature delivery by one iteration.

- *Detailed documentation:* Some features undergo multiple designs and re-designs during an iteration such that people writing the documentation will not be able to finish before the end of the iteration. As documentation is part of done-done feature development, the best choice again is to deliver features one iteration later. Tests can be run and the customer can provide feedback at the end of the current iteration, but the features will only be done-done at the end of the next iteration when the documentation has been finished. In other instances, required documentation may be too detailed and regulated to complete by the end of the iteration—for example, with U.S. government Food and Drug Administration (FDA) projects, which require comprehensive documentation.

- *Special environment:* Many times the development environment differs from the one for testing, integration, and even more so from the production environment. In the production environment you will often find different hardware or different data records which might have a negative impact on the system. Ideally the test or integration environment resembles the production environment and allows testing the system under realistic conditions. In some cases such an environment isn't available at all or only during sparse times. This leads also to delivery delays.

Delaying delivery is never a good idea—agility depends on

---

[8]C. Larman, *Agile and Iterative Development: A Manager's Guide* (Reading, Mass.: Addison-Wesley, 2004).

developers obtaining feedback as quickly as possible—but it is sometimes unavoidable. Whenever it seems that delayed delivery is necessary, find the root cause and look for ways to eliminate the problem and keep to the goal of done-done feature delivery at the end of each iteration. Only if you have no other choice, accept the strategy of delaying delivery.

6.2 Releases

Realistically then, although features theoretically could be delivered to the customer at the end of every iteration, they often are not. Delivering done-done features or rather a feature pack that is meaningful to the customer for review at latest every three months is my recommended practice, with the caveat that developers obtain feedback at each iteration's end from as many testers, domain experts, stakeholders, and customers as feasible. Combined into what is called a *release,* the number of iterations that are delivered together can vary depending on the project and the customer, as shall be addressed in the sections that follow.

Release Iteration

In order to organize a system in a state such that it can be delivered to a customer, some teams require that separate "release iterations" be prepared, which consolidate features and deliverables developed during multiple previous iterations but which, unlike a regular iteration, do not permit time for their own new development. A better approach is taken by teams that organize their system so that, at the end of any iteration, it always is in a state that it can be shipped to the customer if demanded, a practice eliciting more, valuable feedback.

Reasons such as those resulting in delivery delays may make putting a separate release iteration together necessary, but most of the time, the reason is lack of discipline in the team. For example, it could be that although parameters define what puts a feature in the done-done state, such parameters are not widely accepted. Teams might deliver features with flaws (missing documentation or some tests, for example). In such a case, a release iteration is actually a smell signaling a greater problem.

The inherent complexity of a feature may also hinder a team's ability to ship before it has been able to prepare a release iteration. For example, on some of my projects developing embedded applications, other teams developed the hardware for the application. Because the hardware teams had a much slower rhythm than we had, at the end of an iteration we deployed our software either on an older version of the hardware or on a simulator. However, neither of those two deployments would have been tolerable by the customer as a shippable product. When we actually delivered the system, we needed to deploy our software on the newly built hardware, which we only received for the release iteration. On other projects, a release iteration helped because we needed to test our system in a different environment than we normally had available. This environment was too expensive to access every iteration. Thus, we planned and utilized a release iteration to test the system in that special environment.

Release Site

On projects requiring a release iteration, it is good practice to have each team that contributes to the delivery of the release support the integrity and readiness of the final release with at least one representative. I've found that collocating representatives at one location helps to ensure completion of the system and improves project success. It also can work if representatives meet virtually, say, via a telephone conference call, although different time zones may make this approach more difficult than actually getting people together in person.

As with all get-together locations, the release site is never a fixed location but is changed for every release, thereby facilitating mutual respect and trust among all project members and avoiding misbalances in travel efforts, because with every change in the location different team members must travel.

6.3 Integration and Build

Features should be in a delivery-ready, done-done state at the end of every iteration. This state implies that all of the to-be-delivered, completed features are integrated in one coherent system, and are not scattered throughout different variations of the system. Unless there is only one coherent working system, people can never be sure what state the system really is in, and will be distracted from their real work worrying about how much time will be required at the end of the project to combine the different systems into one deliverable. Having one coherent running system additionally provides a major measure of project status. Integrating a system as features are completed is called *continuous integration,* and should be a primary goal for every agile team.

Local Success First

Integration is the moment when the whole development effort comes together. Unfortunately, success in integration doesn't come easily or for free. Considerable cost and effort must be expended early in and throughout a project's lifetime in order to facilitate a smooth integration and build process, especially so on distributed projects. A big mistake I've seen distributed projects make is to ignore the fact that their integration effort does not work properly at one site even *before* extending the project across the globe. Problems grow exponentially worse once a project is expanded to multiple sites, and the longer people wait to address such problems, the more costly and difficult they get to resolve. Moreover, it is very problematic to solve problems originating at one site later on when they impact multiple sites.

Thus, integration problems always deserve the highest priority.

Integration Effort

Jakobsen reports how his company tracks its integration effort: ". . . we automatically collect the time it takes from a build fail until it is fixed again. Developers will have a red icon on their desktop indicating that the last build has failed. The policy is to keep fix time after failed build below 8 working hours."[9]

Integration and build are so important to the success of a distributed project that a minimum of 10 percent of the development effort should be assigned to the task.[10] For example, if thirty people are implementing features, at least three full-time

---

[9]C. Jakobsen, personal communication.
[10]J. Eckstein, op. cit., p. 101.

people should dedicate 100 percent of their time to integration and build.

On many of my projects, we find it works best to have a separate team responsible for integration and build (which includes, as well, conducting integration and smoke tests[11]). This separate team works like a regular feature team, estimating its tasks, planning its iterations, and measuring its velocity. The major difference distinguishing it from other feature teams is that it is okay to interrupt these team members during an iteration, whereas other teams should not accept interruptions (they can deal with changes when planning the next iteration). Interruptions are a high priority for integration teams because their primary task is to ensure a working build.

It is important to understand that having full-time responsibility ". . . does not mean that the integration team would be the only team responsible for integration. Integration should always be the responsibility of all team members. Each team has to integrate its own development effort both internally and with the teams on which it depends."[12] So the integration team's main task is to optimize the integration and build process and not outperform the integration and build itself. For example, very often one of the bottlenecks are check-out times, it is the integration team's task to look for possibilities how to speed those up. Integration teams are most often dispersed, because, typically, problems with integration aren't limited to one site only and cannot be solved by one site.

On some projects, I have the integration team set up as a virtual team and make dedicated members of regular feature teams responsible for integration and build. Those team members have a frequent exchange among themselves, assuring that they are all part of the virtual integration and build team. On other projects, I have worked with feature team members taking turns fulfilling integration and build team roles for a finite time (for instance, one iteration). This can work as well, especially if team members are familiar with the project's integration and build tools and these are working perfectly. However, training every project member to handle specialized functions of integration and build is more difficult than relying on a smaller, dedicated group. While we would always like everyone working on the

---

[11]A smoke test ensure that the system is generally working and does not crash right after the start for example.

[12]Ibid., p. 100.

project to know everything, such a desire is understandably unrealistic.

Production Shut-Down

During integration and build, there is *always* something that can be optimized, but fixing a problem means that the production system comes to a halt. Think of an assembly line shutting down: An integration problem or a slow build puts a hold on the whole project. Some circumstances justify stopping the assembly line, but problems multiply if the stoppage isn't fixed quickly.

I worked on a distributed project with forty developers divided between four sites that struggled tremendously with integration problems. The major reason was that only one person's time was dedicated 100-percent to integration. Two additional team members supported him, but they split their time between integration and development. Although this project required four team members dedicated full-time to integration and build, only one and a half people took charge of this important task.

What often happens in cases like this—when an entire project grinds to a halt—is that managers think the solution is to add manpower to speed development. Their rationale is that the project stopped making measurable progress, and progress normally means implementing features. In this case, we had to *reduce* the development effort and increase integration and build to correct production reliability. Thus sometimes you have to slow down in order to go faster.

Integration and Build Optimization

I have seen too often projects, large and/or distributed, ignore the importance of integration and build. Sometimes, people believe that integration and build only merits attention during a specific part of the project. But if iterations are the heartbeat of a project, integration and build is the heart itself. Integration and build under no circumstances should be taken lightly at any point during the project's lifetime.

With integration and build defined as the heart of the project, all necessary tools for performing integration and build should be accessible to every team member, independent of where the team member is located. Although this might sound like an obvious requirement, every so often I detect life-threatening problems at remote sites (for example, a rigid firewall, conflicting licensing strategies, or inadequate bandwidth). I highly recommend defining accessibility and workability throughout the project infrastructure as the goal for the first global iteration.

The Heartbeat of the Project

Teams must maintain integration and build quality. Problems will occur and intensify over time as development output grows. A build may suddenly take twice as long as in the previous iteration. Most often, you will see that if the build and/or integration time takes "too long," people avoid integrating their effort into the whole system. This leads in turn to even longer build times because now more changes have to be integrated at once. Never underestimate the importance of continually optimizing the integration and build process.

6.4 Infrastructure

To successfully deliver a working system, project members need an environment that enables them to do their work. This is the reason I want to repeat the corresponding agile principle, "Build projects around motivated individuals. Give them the environment and support they need, and trust them to get the job done."[13]

A functioning agile team will assume responsibility for and

---

[13]Agile Manifesto online: http://agilemanifesto.org/principles.html.

ownership of its infrastructure. Such a team doesn't want to be blocked by environmental dysfunction and will maintain a working infrastructure rather than rely on other departments to do so for it. Some companies or sites inhibit this kind of responsibility and team pride by enforcing irrelevant or bureaucratic policies.

It is helpful if knowledgeable people from one site provide support to the other sites facing infrastructure difficulties. Be aware that this can be rather complicated, because infrastructure people often do not officially belong to the project structure, which might restrict access to them. Develop persistence and creativity, and enlist management support, to enable teams at all sites. On one project, for example, the manager decided to pay for infrastructure support out of the project budget, and enabled the project to directly hire the necessary skilled people, understanding that the company had corresponding departments in place and would not put its budget behind our infrastructure needs.

Build and Integration Process and Tools

On regular agile teams (that is one team sitting locally together), team members all refer to the same code base. They most often follow two courses of action: They rebuild the system whenever they've finished a task, resulting in several builds per day (called a *continuous build)*, or they collect all their development effort and start the build at the end of each workday (called a *daily build)*.

Fowler suggests locating the build server wherever most developers are situated.[14] However, this strategy only works if the developers are not evenly spread throughout the different sites. Remember that even with a cluster of developers at one location, other sites need to access the build server regularly, which can delay builds.

Agile teams usually break down builds into several steps—as described below with examples based on a Java environment and supported manually or by automated tools such as those cited:

- *Versions:* Whenever a developer finishes a task, he or she checks the newly created or changed code into the common code base. Typically, this means that a new version

---

[14]M. Fowler, loc. cit.

of this piece of code is created, for instance, by using a tool like Subversion or Git.[15]

- *System build:* Once a new or changed piece of code is checked into the common code base, the whole system will be compiled (and may possibly be linked—depending on the programming language used). Standard tools for building the system is Ant or Maven.[16]
- *Unit and integration tests:* After system build, all unit tests, followed by integration tests, will be executed to ensure that new or changed code and interfaces work as planned in the system. JUnit[17] is very often used for writing and executing unit and integration tests.
- *Smoke test run:* Once unit and integration tests indicate a working system, perform a smoke test to check that the system starts up without any problems and doesn't crash. Smoke tests are normally performed manually.[18]
- *Other tests:* Finally, using automated tests as much as possible, perform additional functional tests and system tests to check the functional correctness of the system.

The first three steps—creating a new version, building the system, and performing unit and integration tests—are usually done automatically by an integration tool, like CruiseControl or Hudson.[19] Schedule these steps either whenever somebody checks revised or new code into the versioning and configuration management tool, or according to a predetermined timeframe (for instance, every ten minutes). If a problem occurs during this process, the tool will identify it.

This build and integration process may sound simple, but be aware that, as Sandberg and Skår point out, "It's not a problem to have a continuous build on a large team, but continuous integration is very difficult."[20]

---

[15] Subversion (OpenSource) on the web http://subversion.tigris.org/, Git (OpenSource) on the web: http://git-scm.com/

[16] Ant (Opensource) on the web: http://ant.apache.org/, Maven on the web: http://maven.apache.org/

[17] JUnit on the web: http://www.junit.org/

[18] For more on smoke tests, see S. McConnell, "Best Practices: Daily Build and Smoke Tests," *IEEE Software,* Vol. 13, No. 4 (July 1996), pp. 143-44.

[19] For CruiseControl, see http://cruisecontrol.sourceforge.net, Hudson (Open-Source) on the web: https://hudson.dev.java.net/

[20] J.-E. Sandberg and L.A. Skår, "Can Agile Practices Deliver High-Quality Large-Scale Offshored Projects?" *Proceedings of XP 2007* (Como, Italy, 2007).

Dedicate several people to continuously improve the integration and build process, and especially focus on making integration work locally first. Very often, global teams benefit from a two-step integration approach, integrating locally before integrating globally. One simple reason to do so is that sometimes bandwidth is inadequate to locally integrate every bit of changed code globally. Dispersed and distributed teams should follow a staged integration strategy by integrating locally and continuously during their workday (first stage) and globally at the end of their workday (second stage) in terms of a daily build.

Configuration Management

Ideally, have one coherent code base in place that every project member can work on. This code base has to be able to version every piece of code and configure different versions (also known as *labeling*). Versioning and labeling are standard function for almost every configuration management tool, but such tools generally do not scale well in a distributed setting. Often the problem is that the configuration management tool might only work well if the project uses the tool's predefined process, which is often not supportive for the distributed setup. According to Estublier, the majority of existing configuration management tools cannot adequately scale for use on distributed projects.[21] Distributed teams need tools that support a flexible process. Thus, I highly recommend vetting tools at the very beginning of the project, to address each tool's suitability.[22]

Several global teams report good experiences using the configuration management tool Subversion.[23] Global projects' success with the configuration management tool apparently correlates to their ability to maintain bandwidth to support fast, efficient access to their code base. Often it turns out that it is much too slow. This needs to be addressed by replicating the actual code base on a local server at each site and synchronizing those replicas as often as possible—ideally, automatically. Despite the reported success, I recommend using this strategy for emergen-

---

[21] J. Estublier, "Software Configuration Management: A Roadmap," *Proceedings of the Conference on the Future of Software Engineering* (Limerick, Ire., 2000), pp. 279-99.

[22] For more on starting a project, see Chapter 10, "Introducing Agility into New and Existing Projects."

[23] For Subversion, see http://subversion.tigris.org/.

cies only because of the possibility of mismatching replicated versions and introducing currency errors into the system.

Which configuration management tools to vet may depend on a project's stage in its evolutionary global development effort.[24] For fully centralized development (stage I), tools like Visual Source Safe are typically in use.[25] For centrally coordinated global development (stage II), concurrent approaches like Subversion are more appropriate. Finally, for globally integrated development, fully distributed development systems like Mercurial and Git are appropriate.[26]

Ideally, as Nessier describes, code base turnover follows the sun: ". . . the India team takes ownership for the code base in their morning, and hands over the code base to the U.S. team at the end of the day with a successful build."[27] In order to support this approach, choose a configuration management tool that allows all project members to access the actual code base, either directly, or, less advisedly, by replicating it.

Fowler recommends the following versioning practice: "...if you commit changes . . . you should not go home until you have received the email message from CruiseControl that says that your changes resulted in a successful build. A late night bad build is much more serious when the remote office is running off the same build."[28]

> **Follow the Sun by Joseph Pelrine**[a]
>
> For me, the big challenge in doing multi-site, distributed development does not have to do with the technical side of things, but rather how to build trust and respect between people who may never meet each other in person. This

---

[24]Thanks to Jamie Allsop for pointing out the evolutionary reflection aspect. For a refresher on evolutionary stages, refer back to the section entitled "Centrally Coordinated or Globally Integrated" in Chapter 2.

[25]Visual Source Safe (VSS) is a propietary version control system from Microsoft.

[26]Mercurial and Git both are free, distributed-version-control systems. For Mercurial on the web, see http://www.selenic.com/mercurial/. For Git on the web, see http://git.or.cz/.

[27]R. Nessier, "Go Global! Translate the Proven Benefits of Agile Development to a Distributed Team Environment," *Agile Development* (Spring 2007), pp. 7-10.

[28]M. Fowler, op. cit., p. 3.

lack of trust slows the development process drastically, because teams sometimes spend more time checking other teams' code (to ensure its quality) than doing development themselves.

I saw this problem while implementing a 24/5 follow-the-sun XP/Scrum development setup for a client, and found the solution to be strict adherence to a few generally agreed-upon rules. The teams rigorously followed all eXtreme programming practices, writing all production code in pairs, doing test-driven development, and constantly refactoring code to keep it as simple as possible. Coding standards were agreed upon and strictly enforced, and were checked automatically as part of the continuous integration process. When asked, all team members confirmed that these practices alone helped them go faster, because they could relax in the knowledge that everyone else was being just as strict.

The various teams' working hours dovetailed into each other, and work was coordinated in "handover" meetings—a type of distributed Daily Scrum, where the team handing over reported on what it did during the past day, and the team being handed to reported on what it would do during the coming day. After the meeting, the team being handed to quickly wrote up notes on the meeting in a wiki. I normally don't like people keeping written protocols of such meetings (it often implies a blame-driven culture), but we found that a little written documentation was useful to avoid the "Chinese whispers" or "broken telephone" breakdown of information flow while passing through teams around the world.

The one technique that made the process click, though, was the team's Golden Rule: At the end of a workday, all code was checked into the source control repository, all tests ran green, the build worked, and the build time was under 10 minutes—or you threw it all away, and rolled back to the last version of the baseline that met all these conditions. If that meant that you threw away a whole day's work, then tough luck—you *never* passed a broken code base on to another team.

[a]Joseph Pelrine (Switzerland), European Agile Pioneer.

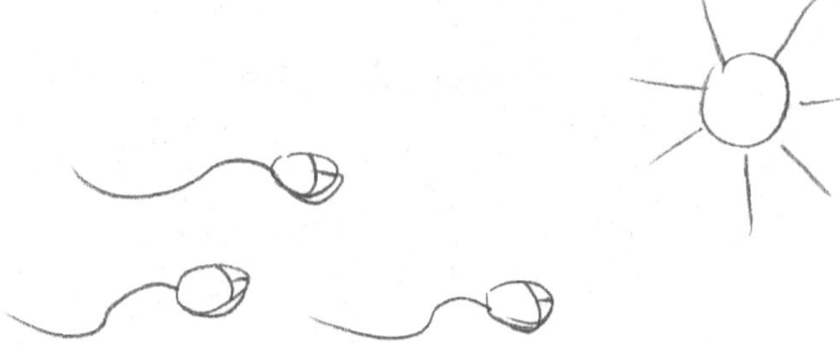

Follow the Sun

Power

Technical breakdowns, like power outages, can be problematic at some sites. Unfortunately, there is no real resolution to a challenge like this, other than escalating the problem and "hoping" for the best. Depending on how often such breakdowns occur, distributed projects can either try to plan for schedule slippage caused by regular outages by reducing the velocity for the affected teams, work around short-term outages by providing notebook computers with batteries to frequently affected sites, or consider moving the whole team to a different site that doesn't regularly experience breakdowns. The latter option means exchanging one challenge for another—introducing the difficulties of travel, extra costs, and social disconnection, to name a few.

Security

Some sites and companies have an obstructive security philosophy that may hinder development progress. On several of my projects, one or more sites' firewall prevented access to the shared code base or configuration system because the firewall didn't allow access and the philosophy didn't allow change. Kircher, et al., describe a similar experience on a project distributed between Germany, India, Italy, and the United States: "As Prashant [Jain] had to work most of the time from behind a firewall [in India], he was not able to connect to the team repository directly. Other team members had to send him snapshots of the code via e-mail. This process was tedious and error-prone."[29]

On one project where I encountered the firewall problem, all sites actually belonged to the same company, yet we still faced this problem for which thus far we have not found a satisfactory solution. To work around it on one project, we e-mailed changes to the code base back and forth (you can imagine how cumbersome this exchange was); on other projects, we used more-open ports of the intranet to overcome the security problem. Bas Vodde shares his insight on the subject: ". . . security measures often lead to a totally baleful mindset in product development so that security is more often harmful than beneficial. This is especially true in an agile environment, since it prevents learning and adaptation."[30]

Very often, the best solution is to alter existing infrastructure so that it is less restrictive. Sangwan, et al., report first using a configuration management tool that didn't work well over public and medium-bandwidth network connections, and then "realized the importance of the software configuration management infrastructure and decided to port to the Subversion revision control system, allowing access to the repository over standard HTTP and having the advantage of accessibility even in restricted network environments."[31] As a consequence, balance thoroughly simplification of the development with the necessary security.

Network Sense

Although not as much a hindrance on one of my recent distributed projects as the infrastructure problems discussed above, but more an annoyance, is having to change the network masks (IP addresses) every time we move from one site to another because all project networks are set up differently. This step is not difficult to do, but it is annoying because it also requires people not working on a Unix platform to reboot whenever accessing the network from a different location. It only takes

---

[29]M. Kircher, P. Jain, A. Corsaro, and D. Levine, "Distributed Extreme Programming," in M. Marchesi, G. Succi, D. Wells, and L. Williams, *Extreme Programming Perspectives*, (Upper Saddle River, N.J.: Pearson Education, 2002), p. 567.

[30]B. Vodde, personal communication.

[31]R. Sangwan, et al., op. cit., p. 163.

a pinch of commonsense to know that the problem never arises if the networks are set up similarly at all involved sites.

Also commonsense on large distributed projects is ensuring that network capacity can accommodate the project's network traffic. I recommend equipping the project network with a high capability early on rather than waiting for problems to manifest, and possibly interrupt or derail critically timed activities such as shipping a release.

Tools

Simplify distributed development by having the same versions of the same tools available at all sites. On several projects, we succeeded with different development environments because we harmonized the way the development environments stored code in a common, versioned, code base. As another example, a project might either prohibit using a tool's tabulator key or set each site's tools so that using the tabulator key results in the same predefined number of blanks everywhere (which it does normally not and which leads to unreadable code).

Using the same tool versions at all locations is essential, especially in terms of compilers when programming in a language like C++ that needs to be compiled. Otherwise, the system is likely to work at one location but not at another.

6.5 Summary

To ensure timely deliverables and to elicit valuable feedback, teams need to leverage iterations using a regular, steady rhythm, as in a heartbeat. Synchronize iteration length and schedule, as different time zones allow, in combination with all members' joint understanding of what is done-done to build a working system at the end of every iteration.

Although every iteration ideally should produce a usable system, some projects may decide to plan a release iteration that will ensure a product's readiness to ship. Release iterations should follow the same heartbeat as any other iteration. Moreover, establish a release site at which all teams or representatives of all teams that contribute to the release iteration work together to finish and install the product jointly. Be sure as well to rotate release site locations.

If iterations are the heartbeat, then integration and build is the heart of the project. Only after integration and build will the goal of one coherent system be feasible. Very often, the importance and required effort of having a smooth integration and build globally in place is undervalued. Projects must verify that integration works well locally before growing the project globally. Put any integration and build problem on high priority, because a flawed or failed integration and build puts a project in a position comparable to an assembly line on hold.

Depending on a project's distribution of teams and global infrastructure, project members might work on a local code base during the workday and only integrate into the global code base at the end of their day. Most infrastructure issues that sometimes slow down a distributed project typically relate to cumbersome policies.

7. Ensuring Business Value

Everything with value must come to light.

— Johann Wolfgang von Goethe

As has been stated in prior chapters, a primary goal of agile development is to ensure the greatest possible business value for the customer. The Agile Manifesto mandates: "Our highest priority is to satisfy the customer through early and continuous delivery of valuable software."[1] However, it is important to note that agile development is not about merely delivering some level of business value; it is about delivering the *highest* level of business value that can be achieved at the given time. Especially on large, globally distributed projects, the risk is high that team members will focus on early and continuous delivery of all kinds of ingenious bells and whistles, but will overlook the opportunity to produce practical components offering the greatest business value to the customer.

7.1 Steering Through Valuable Features

Feature teams navigate through development based on customer specifications and requirements. A member of the feature team, the domain expert helps teams to understand the customers' desired business functionality and works with the testers to verify that it is achieved. How the large, global team is structured ensures that feature teams care for the completion and delivery of this functionality, but it is the customer alone who determines which business functionality will provide the highest business value at a particular moment. That is to say, the customer or its designated representative or—to use the Scrum term—the product owner steers feature teams according

---

[1] Agile Manifesto online: http://agilemanifesto.org/principles.html.

to whatever business functionality needs to be built in what order.

Therefore, the product owner needs to have an overview over all required functionalities and communicate their order of priority to the relevant feature teams. In response, the feature teams will need to provide feedback on how many features they can deliver per iteration (which can differ from feature team to feature team), as well as note throughout development whether any features are left over from past iterations and will need to be reprioritized. Thus, the product owner ensures maximum business value by steering the iterations through features, and, at the end of each iteration, decides whether delivered features are fully acceptable or need to be reworked.

Real-Customer Awareness

If whoever are the real customers is represented by another entity as product owner, the parties must regularly exchange priority-status updates so as to maintain focus on what provides the highest possible business value to the real customers at any moment. Decisions must be based not on the representative's perceptions or assumptions about priority, but on the real customers' absolute selection, making it essential that the product owner has direct interaction with the real customers. The product owner, therefore, needs a clear and direct line of communication with the customers, but also should fully understand every aspect relating to the real customers' business.

The relationship between the real customers and the product owner both has to be established and then nurtured throughout the project's lifetime. By regularly inviting the real customers to project sites to see progress firsthand, the product owner can obtain feedback on features under development. Of similar value are product owner visits at customer site(s). In this way, all parties gain a better understanding of how well the system under development will deliver business value to the real customers.

Connecting to a Distant Customer by Daniel Karlström[a]

Customer-handling in globally distributed projects is made difficult chiefly by the reduced opportunity for direct communication. Any opportunity for communication with the customer therefore becomes crucial, and the quality of that communication will often make or break the project.

The customer is the only stakeholder that knows what needs to be done. The saying "the customer is always right" seems especially appropriate for software projects. What the customer does not know is how the desired functionality is to be implemented and the limitations of the technology in use. It is of paramount importance to manage the customer's expectations as to what is feasible as early as possible. In our projects, this involves setting expectations with regard to the quality of graphic design, performance aspects, the number of compatible devices, etc. Over-promising in a conceptual or even pre-closing phase will cause problems when the achievable product is demonstrated, either at delivery or early in the development process.

As time passes, the customer gains knowledge not only regarding how the desired functionality can be implemented, but also how the functionality works in practice—and the idea of what is really wanted evolves. The developers are chiefly learning what the customer wants, but also gaining knowledge of how to better implement that functionality. This continuing evolution of the project helps produce the best possible final product, but requires a very good relationship not only communication-wise between customer and developers, but also a very trusting business relationship between the customer organization and the delivering organization.

All stakeholders must realize that changes to initially proposed functionality can result in an improved final product, but will probably also incur increased development costs as well as cause the project to run later than initially planned. Each modification request must therefore be evaluated by the customer with this trade-off in mind. It would be wise to plan for such occurrences from the beginning of the project, although the need for changes is not apparent at this stage and the customer is usually very sure of what it thinks it wants. Any sign of scope flexibility in the propositioning phase can be seen as a weakness by some customers.

This complete learning process must be facilitated continuously during the course of the project through frequent communication via any available means. In a non-distributed project, this would preferably be iteration meetings between customer and developer or even by having the customer on site à la XP. In distributed development, this is possible, so substitutes such as e-mail, VOIP, or video conference (even though bandwidth concerns mean this is not possible from our office in Cambodia) need to be utilized to their full potential. We run voice status meetings between critical project functions on a daily basis and most developers have chat windows open with the sales team contact and/or the end customer for the project they are currently working on, whenever it is possible. This has lead to information sometimes being shared more easily across continents than across the office table.

For a globally distributed project, if budget allows, we find setting up an initial meeting between technical and customer representatives to be advantageous. What is decided and planned at this meeting is of less importance than fostering a good working relationship that following communications can build on. The specification will always evolve, but this will not be done effectively if the customer and the technical team do not have a good working relationship. Hitting a stationary target is comparatively easy; just aim and fire. It is hitting the moving targets that is difficult. In most of our projects, the target moves very rapidly, and failing to adjust means missing the mark. It is worse to deliver the wrong product than to deliver nothing at all, even if that delivery is what was agreed on at the start of the project.

In one of our projects that involved a customer proxy, we identified feedback cycles of several days due to unfortunate time zones and inbox-checking frequency. At the time, some of these cycles represented a time period the same order of magnitude as the remaining time to delivery, so some short-circuiting was absolutely necessary. Our optimal configuration is for the customer and technical representatives to talk directly about functionality, but to also have a sales contact appointed with whom the customer can discuss business concerns and obtain explanations of developers' technical jargon. Sometimes, a customer proxy is absolutely necessary—a customer may be inaccessible or the application may be written in a language different from that used by the development team—but we try to avoid this as much as possible.

Given the project members' reduced ability to communicate in a globally distributed project, agile values become more important. They promote continuous communication and eliminate misunderstandings throughout the project, not just at the beginning and end.

[a]Daniel Karlström (Cambodia) is COO and founder of Golden Gekko Ltd.

Iteration Preparation

On small, collocated teams, the product owner typically spends most of the time during an iteration helping the team and only a few hours at the end of that iteration preparing for the following one. This approach works on a small project because, by working so closely with the team, the product owner knows exactly what it will deliver and therefore what can be planned for delivery in the next iteration. It is also relatively simple for the product owner to keep the big picture in mind, because, with only one team, the project's progress toward its goal is straightforward.

The approach described above, unfortunately, does not scale well for a large, global team. Working closely with one feature team, a product owner on a large, global team undoubtedly knows what value that feature team can deliver, but knowing the expected delivery of other feature teams on the same project might influence how priorities for the single feature team are set. Therefore, continuous coordination among all product owners is critical to success on large, distributed projects, and means that product owners must dedicate more time to preparing the next iteration than they do in a collocated setting.

Product owners must ensure that feature development follows a logical progression—one team's feature development effort should be independent of all other teams'. Most of the time, the very structure of a large, global team that is divided into small, focused feature teams will eliminate dependencies among the diverse feature teams. As Sandberg and Skår observe, "If you find it difficult to do first things first because of dependencies between teams, you probably have the wrong team structure."[2]

---

[2]J.-E. Sandberg and L.A. Skår, op. cit.

If dependencies between planned features are evident, reconsider team structure to take those dependent features into account in the planning. Go back and re-plan feature development not only according to business-value priorities, but also with dependencies in mind to ensure that features that depend on one another either are not planned in the same timeframe or are assigned to the same feature team.

If neither of these approaches seems feasible, product owners, together with the architect(s), need to identify dependencies and plan for their co-development during the next few iterations. Cohn calls this strategy "a rolling lookahead plan" and defines the practice thusly: "A rolling lookahead plan simply looks forward a small number of iterations (typically, only two to three) and allows teams to coordinate work by sharing information about what each will be working on in the near future."[3]

Although product owners may not be in favor of this activity because devising a lookahead plan to deal with interdependent-feature-development across different teams, keeping the plan up-to-date, and continuously monitoring its feasibility can cost them dearly in terms of time, the approach can be viable way for projects to prepare iterations.

For most projects that need to take interdependent-feature-development into account, we typically hold what we call "a pre-planning meeting" in the middle of an iteration in order to begin preparing for the next iteration. At this meeting, participants strive to identify features that cannot be delivered at the end of the current iteration and pre-select features for the next iteration by respecting possible dependencies among those features. Later on, feature teams use information gathered during the pre-planning meeting to plan the next iteration in detail.

The pre-planning meeting is facilitated by the lead product owner and is attended by product owners as well as by the architect (or architects, if the project is large enough to merit more than one architect) who ensures that technical dependencies are not missed. For example, a technical dependency that the architect might note could be that it is more feasible to develop feature B before feature A. If the lead product owner respects this argument, development of feature A will be postponed until a future iteration. Another technical observation might note

---

[3]M. Cohn, *Agile Estimating and Planning* (Boston: Addison-Wesley, 2006), p. 210.

that because feature C, say, is a technical derivative compatible with feature B, it would make sense to have the team working on feature B also work on feature C. Regardless of whatever arguments favor the selection of one feature over another one during the pre-planning meeting, the final decision about which features to develop in the next iteration is always made by the lead product owner, generally in consultation with the team of product owners or rather the business side, because, as the Agile Manifesto records, consideration of what has the greatest value to the customer takes precedence.

In addition to the pre-selected features and (if applicable) an updated rolling lookahead plan, the outcome of the pre-planning meeting is a first draft of acceptance criteria for each pre-selected feature for the upcoming iteration.

The information garnered in pre-planning meetings helps team members identify dependencies between features and as well enables feature teams to accelerate iteration planning as distributed project work continues.

Taking into account the considerable amount of work product owners must expend during one iteration to oversee planning for the subsequent iteration, it is no wonder that large, distributed projects commonly call upon domain experts to serve as feature-team members, supporting the teams by clarifying features during each iteration—as will be illustrated in the following section.

Understanding Requirements

On distributed projects following a traditional linear approach, parties specify and sign off on product requirements not only before anyone begins design or writes code, but also at a different location than the site or sites at which the requirements specification will be translated into product. The premise is that the requirements can be specified in such a way that ambiguity is completely eliminated and thus the implementation exactly matches the specification.

Of course, completely eliminating ambiguity regarding requirements is impossible, particularly if the analysts who write up the specification come from one cultural background and the people implementing the spec come from another. The importance of someone's cultural background cannot be overstated: It is the basis for how people understand and interpret the world about them, and is one reason why cultural differences among teams and even teammates on agile projects must be squarely addressed. The people with knowledge about a domain must work closely with the people realizing the domain to assure that everyone shares the same vision and has the same understanding. This is the reason why the product owner has to work together with the feature team and why it is important for teams to deliver working software with every iteration and to ask product owners to provide feedback.[4]

Another problem inherent in signed-and-sealed specifications prepared on distributed projects that use a traditional linear approach is that most of the time that is spent in requirements analysis is for naught. The reason is simple: Requirements change, sometimes slowly over time, sometimes so rapidly that what is required today is not the same as what will be a must-have requirement tomorrow. And what the customer wants in the end is hardly the same thing as was deemed an absolute requirement at the beginning of the project. Agile methods, therefore, save this valuable time and clarify only requirements relevant to current iterations' feature development, giving highest priority to ensuring the greatest possible business value for the customer.

Treating Documentation as Requirements

For a feature to be considered in the done-done state, it must be documented.[5] Documentation for some project environments, however, includes more than just feature documentation. Agile projects always consider whether requests for additional documentation will provide business value or are simply creating waste. For example, on a project regulated by the Food and Drug Administration, from an agile perspective FDA-required documentation is treated the same way any other requirement is treated because it is clear that the FDA is a stakeholder of the project and that delivering all documentation required by the FDA will increase business value. Thus, the product owner must balance the different needs of diverse stakeholders (including the FDA) and prioritize the requirements accordingly.

---

[4] For more on product-owner collaboration, see Chapter 3, "Building Teams."

[5] For the concept of done-done, see Chapter 6, "Ensuring Development and Delivery."

In some instances, requested documentation is directly connected to a feature and its inclusion will mark the feature as done-done, but finishing all the accompanying documentation within the same timeframe as the feature may not be feasible unless delivery is delayed[6].

7.2 Team Velocity

When beginning a new project with a new team or introducing an agile approach to a project that has previously used traditional, linear development methods, it is difficult to develop a plan for even the first iteration, let alone for an entire project, because there is neither a track record nor baseline data upon which to chart feature-delivery velocity. If pressed to come up with an overall project plan before conducting the first iteration, I recommend estimate schedule and deliverables for only the first iteration, and then use the estimated numbers to forecast the rest of the project. Be aware, however, that numbers projected for the first iteration especially are probably not very accurate, and should be adapted or replaced as real data are obtained. Upon completion of each iteration, revisit the overall plan to more accurately plan the next iteration, and update the overall project plan regularly, optimally after each iteration.

If possible, develop the overall project plan only after two or three iterations have been completed. It shouldn't take a rocket scientist to conclude that waiting to incorporate several iterations' feature-delivery data will make the project plan much more realistic than can be accomplished by estimate-based forecasting.

Unknown Velocity

Still, the problem remains: How can a plan for the first iteration even be estimated if the team's velocity is unknown? My answer: It cannot be planned with any real accuracy, but we begin by breaking the selected features into smaller tasks, and then estimate those tasks (in hours). We include team members'

---

[6]For delaying the delivery, see Chapter 6 in chapter 6, "Ensuring Development and Delivery."

projected availability for this iteration as additional input data, but I recognize that team members, like most people, usually state "available time" more as ideal and not as real time.

Ideal time is the period during which a team is available for project work, calculated in terms of working hours without interruption. *Real time* accounts for and deducts the time people need for all kinds of "distractions", for example, answering e-mails, the phone, questions from their peers, and so on. Use real time to estimate a team's velocity, although later on the actual velocity will of course be based on delivery of business value using Yesterday's Weather[7] rather than on available time. My rule of thumb is to compute real time from ideal time by dividing by a factor of two and half. Consider a team of three people. The team has agreed on an iteration length of one workweek. Assuming all team members will be available full-time, the ideal time would be three (people) multiplied by five (days)—fifteen ideal days. Dividing the ideal fifteen by my factor of two and a half leaves the team with six real days. Thus, this team will only plan tasks for the total of six days.

---

[7]More on realistic planning, see chapter 4 "Communication and Trust."

Yesterday's Weather

At the end of the iteration, team members analyze what they were able to deliver and use that data as their velocity for the next iteration. Subsequent iterations use the team's velocity which is based on what is delivered rather than on calendar time.

Estimation Unit

Many teams estimate features only in the unit of time. Most often, teams (also in non-agile projects) estimate in ideal time because they can't (or don't want to) imagine how much time they will spend on secondary tasks. If this is the case in your setting, for a start you can use my earlier suggestion and use a factor of two and a half. Yet, for more precision you need to figure out what is the individual's team factor between real time and ideal time or rather how much estimated ideal time can this team accomplish in an iteration (which refers to real time). You can do so by simply summing up the estimated (ideal) time of the completed features. So for instance, at the end of a two-week iteration you might find out that your team of five members delivers in this ten weeks of real time (five members multiplied by two weeks equals ten weeks) features which have originally been estimated in total of four weeks (of ideal time).

To avoid confusion associated with these different meanings of time, agile teams often abandon the idea of estimating in time and instead use a measurement system based on a different estimation unit: points. Points can be more precisely identified as feature points, story points, or complexity points, but whatever estimation unit a project selects, it should use the same unit for the entire project.[8] Thus, all feature teams utilize the same estimation unit. On most of my projects, we use complexity points, which estimate the complexity of work that will be required to complete one feature. For example, if feature B appears to be as complex to develop as we've estimated for developing feature A, we set the estimate for B to be the same as that for A. Or if features C and D together appear to be as complex to develop as feature E, we will estimate feature E accordingly.

Agile teams very often estimate features jointly, using a practice called Planning Poker in which team members individually assign point scores to certain features, and then reveal their "hands," discussing scores and reconciling differences of opinion.[9] Discussed at length in the following section, Planning Poker allows participants to evaluate each feature to be developed by an entire project relative to all others and eliminates the distinct possibility that one developer is busy estimating a feature while another developer is actually implementing it. In essence, the practice permits a project-wide overview, revealing each feature in relation to all others.

Although the points system provides a better way to estimate feature development than generally can be estimated using real or ideal time, it does not guarantee accuracy. To add a control at the start of an agile project, establish a common baseline to ensure that everyone on every team on a project evaluates, for

---

[8] For more on story points, see M. Cohn, op. cit., p. 35ff.
[9] Ibid., loc. cit.

instance, eight complexity points in exactly the same way. Although this baseline will shift a bit as each feature team typically estimates its own new or changed features, it nevertheless will provide a valuable measure of desired uniformity.

Planning Poker

A well-accepted technique for coming up with estimates and then in turn with a plan, Planning Poker starts with a product owner presenting feature requirements to a team. Normally referred to simply as "developers," an entire team participates: architects, product owners, analysts, designers, programmers, testers, database experts – just whoever contributes to completing the features. Each developer plays with a deck of cards marked with possible estimation values. As recommended by Cohn, I also recommend starting with the following possible complexity estimation values: 1, 2, 3, 5, and 8, whereby a 1 indicates the least complex, and an 8, the most difficult.[10]

Let's look more closely at what might transpire in Planning Poker: The estimation starts with the product owner briefly presenting a feature. Developers may ask clarifying questions, and then each developer selects one card from his or her deck, holding the card so that the estimation value cannot be seen by the other players. When all developers have selected a card, they simultaneously display the cards for all to view.

A developer who selects, say, a card indicating an estimate of 5 believes that developing the presented feature will be as difficult as developing another feature estimated as a 2 combined with one estimated as a 3. If everyone estimates the same value, the complexity level for developing that feature is recorded and the product owner moves on to present the next feature to be estimated. If some estimates differ, the developers whose estimations are at the extremes explain their reasoning. For example, if the majority of developers estimate complexity as a 5, a person estimating a 1 might explain, "I have implemented a comparable feature, and it was really easy to complete." A person estimating an 8 might reason, "It's probably easy to implement, but it will be exceedingly difficult to test." To move closer toward reaching consensus on the particular feature's complexity level, other players and the product owner can join

---

[10]Loc. cit., p. 56ff.

the discussion to help clarify the various issues. Once discussion has run its course, all developers repeat the process, re-estimating the feature's complexity level until the whole group agrees.[11]

Estimating one feature using the Planning Poker technique typically takes no more than three rounds, but if more rounds are required, we ask the minority if they can support the estimate of the majority. A team should never settle on an estimation value by computing the average of everyone's hand. No team member has suggested the average and thus, computing the average engrains the habit of forfeiting responsibility and investment in decisions and planning. Additionally, although the goal of Planning Poker is to estimate feature complexity, in my experience, a real benefit comes through the discussions about features because they ensure that the whole team reaches the same understanding about each feature's complexity.

Ideally, all members of a dispersed team periodically meet in person to play Planning Poker. Most estimating takes place at the start of the project, at this time the team presumably will be working together at one site.[12] To develop estimates throughout or at later points during the course of the project, traveling to meet in person might not be worth the potential gain for a dispersed team. Instead, teams can conduct Planning Poker virtually, using Web cams or an online version of the game.[13]

Estimation Parity

Most estimating, however, will take place at the beginning of the project and will be conducted by the starting team. By practicing agile methods and Planning Poker at the beginning of the project, the starting team will estimate all known features, thereby creating a baseline for future estimates. Once the project grows, and disperses, questions arise as to who will estimate new or changed features and how they will maintain consistent estimation parameters. Two approaches to addressing these issues are either (1) to form one estimation team at

---

[11]This practice is similar to estimation sessions using the wideband Delphi estimation method—see http://www.stellman-greene.com/aspm/content/view/23/38/.

[12]For more on foundations and setting projects up, see Chapter 10, "Introducing Agility into New and Existing Distributed Projects."

[13]For a free online version of Planning Poker, see http://www.planningpoker.com.

the start of the project that will continue to do all estimating throughout the lifetime of the project, or (2) to pursue individual-team estimations:

- *One estimation team:* After a project scales up, adding more teams, continue to have the original team come together to conduct Planning Poker to estimate new or changed features.
    - The major advantage of this approach is better-aligned estimation values because the estimators have a common understanding about the baseline. In other words, a feature estimated as a 3 later during a project will be as complex as a feature estimated as a 3 at the project's start.
    - The primary disadvantages are that the Planning Poker experience is not shared by the whole team, that the complexity values estimated by the original team might be viewed by the other teams as dead-wrong values forced upon them, and most importantly that the teams implementing these feature didn't develop a joint understanding about their features beforehand by using this estimation technique.
- *Individual-team estimations:* When introducing agile methods and Planning Poker at later points during a project's lifetime, create a conjoint baseline for estimating feature development by bringing together at a single site one or two representatives from each feature team who meet in person and estimate as many features as possible to create a baseline covering a variety of complexities. Representatives then return to their teams and share the baseline and parameters for subsequent estimates to be made by the individual feature team.
    - The significant advantage of this approach is that each team can estimate new or changed features at any time without waiting for the original estimation team to do so. Feature teams following this approach feel not only more ownership of those estimates but also learn about and prepare for feature development at the same time.
    - The primary disadvantage is that typically, after a while, different feature teams interpret the baseline differently. Each feature team will develop a slightly different understanding about what kind of feature is easy to develop and what is difficult.

The best solution can be to combine these two estimation approaches in order to prevent too much baseline deviation. Ask a few people from the original estimation team to take part in sessions held by the individual feature teams. With a combined approach that starts with one estimation team and then, when the project grows globally, switches to individual-team estimations supported by one original estimation team member, a distributed project can achieve constancy and maintain control over delivering value to its customer iteration after iteration.

Velocity Disparity

It usually takes an agile team about three iterations to establish a rhythm of planning–doing–inspecting–adapting. It can take another two iterations to stabilize velocity.

Comparing two teams' velocities is moot because velocity is based on how accurate the estimates prove to be and because no two teams and no two projects will be exactly comparable. For instance, assuming that a high velocity is better than a low velocity can derail an entire project if a team's high velocity is based on very pessimistic estimates and another team's low velocity on very optimistic estimates. The low-velocity team could, in fact, be faster. There will always be unquantifiable differences between individual feature teams, making team-velocity comparisons of little use.

However, it is important to measure the velocity of all teams to gain overall project velocity. For example, if feature team A completes 16 points per iteration, feature team B completes 21, and feature team C completes 13, the sum, indicating overall project velocity, is 50. You can use this velocity to predict the remainder of the project, estimating that each iteration will complete about 50 points. This way, you do not have to calibrate future iterations' points, only make sure that teams perform consistently enough to maintain their velocity. I have always found this sum accurate enough to predict delivery content and schedule.

Observing an individual feature team's velocities can also easily identify a team that is struggling. For instance, the effect of growing a feature team or increasing the dispersion of a feature team is often directly reflected by an oscillation in its velocity. Monitor each team's velocity for any early warning of risk in its meeting estimated feature delivery to the customer.

Just as moot as comparing different team velocities is comparing velocities of individual team members. On my projects, we do not bother calculating the velocity of a specific person; we are only interested in each team's velocity because we need to know if project delivery is at risk or not. Very often, the team members who play the most important roles on the team are unable to complete a single task during an iteration, implying these people have a velocity of zero. This apparent zero velocity is actually due to their role supporting the rest of the team. These team members are often the ones transferring knowledge within the team, and ensuring a common vision and development culture within the team. Although their velocity is zero, their contribution to the project is enormous.

7.3 Planning an Iteration

The product owner steers each iteration by selecting features with the highest business value. The feature team, usually represented by the coach, informs the product owner about outstanding features from the current iteration and any dependencies and technical risks to take into account.

Feature-Planning Integrity

Although each feature team on a project should plan iterations independently, it is up to the product owners and the chief architect to ensure that the different planning efforts will fit together. Plan coordination can be fairly straightforward as there typically is not much interdependence in terms of work between feature teams.

Coordinating planning grows more complex if a project has differently structured teams spread globally, for example with the focus on technical components. Yet even with feature teams in place, ensure that all teams are reachable for example via phone in order to clarify some possible issues immediately during the planning session. But if the difference between time zones is extreme, coordinate planning using a variety of communication media, and schedule planning to take place at (approximately) the same time each session. If a project establishes a universal heartbeat, scheduling iterations in sync with all teams should be feasible.

Planning-Meeting Essentials

Planning meetings work best if members of a feature team meet in person. If this is not possible because the feature team is heavily dispersed, ensure that the team meets in person to plan at least its first two iterations. Thereafter, enable the team to plan jointly from time to time throughout the project (for instance, make every third planning meeting an in-person meeting).

A planning meeting typically starts with the product owner presenting features he or she wishes to have delivered during the next iteration, and then takes questions for clarification. Next, the team breaks these features into more fine-grained tasks and estimates those. Then, led by the coach, the team cross-checks estimated tasks with individual members' availability during the next iteration. The team also computes the total of the features it plans to deliver (in complexity points) and cross-checks this number with the current team velocity. Depending on the results, the members form an agreement about what they believe they can deliver. (This process might require additional negotiation with the product owner.) Consequently, the product owner may add or postpone some features. The feature team concludes the session with an official commitment to features to be delivered by the end of the iteration.

Planning-Meeting Schedule

On one of my projects, we scheduled an in-person planning meeting for the dispersed teams every other iteration. We also rotated planning-meeting locations so as to avoid infringing on just one set of team members' personal lives, making it easier for an ever-changing subset of team members to stay home while somebody else traveled.

Planning Meeting Schedule

For easing traveling we found that it is very helpful if the planning meeting doesn't take place at the start or at the end of the week. Scheduling the planning meeting at the boundaries of the week, requires often that the team members will have to travel during their weekends. However, depending on what kinds of countries are involved in your global development effort, it might be difficult to figure out what the boundaries of the week are. –Not every country (e.g. Israel) understands Monday till Friday as the working week. – So my general advice is to schedule the planning meeting on a day that makes traveling the easiest for your team.

When feature-team members are not able to meet face-to-face, we set up virtual planning meetings, using communication tools like NetMeeting, a wiki, or a Web cam to help members engage one another. We do not restrict ourselves to one communication tool, because we find that conveying different types of information requires that we use different media.

Tangible Planning Tools

I prefer to actually break down a feature into tasks and estimate those using such simple, tangible tools as index cards and sticky notes.[14] I prefer these tangible items to electronic tools because the latter typically require one person to act as scribe through whom other people channel their comments, enabling the scribe alone to control everything that gets recorded! In my view, that's a practice that is neither good nor agile, but an even more significant problem is that planning can't be done in parallel and will take much more time. Also important, as Vodde observes, "energy in the planning will be lower due to the centralized tool; focus is always there" on the tool instead of on the planning.[15]

A dispersed planning meeting, however, must use some electronic tools. I have planned collaboratively using video conferencing for connecting dispersed sites, and have also used a shared whiteboard to simulate tangible tools.[16] This takes much longer, though, than facilitating an in-person planning meeting using tangible tools.

On all of my distributed projects, although we use tangible planning tools, we record the results of meetings electronically. We do so not only for dispersed but even for collocated feature teams on distributed projects because the results are important to a wider audience than the feature team itself. The electronic result—namely, the iteration plan—should be visible, prominent, and easily accessible to everybody on a team. It not only records the outcome of iteration planning but also serves as an iteration-tracking resource.

7.4 Iteration Tracking

The daily synchronization should inform everyone about project status. For instance, a feature team might want to know any of the following[17]:

- Will we be able to deliver the features we promised at the planning meeting?
- How much work do we still have to do?

---

[14] For more on tangible, estimating tools, see M. Cohn, op. cit.

[15] B. Vodde, personal communication.

[16] Thanks to Frank Maurer for sharing this experience. For the shared whiteboard AgilePlanner, see http://ase.cpsc.ucalgary.ca/ase/index.php/AgilePlanning/Home/.

[17] More on the agile practice of daily synchronization in chapter 9, "Customizing Practices."

- Are there possible synergies between tasks?
- Do we need help to complete specific tasks?

Often, the product owner, chief architect, coach, and project manager will also want to know this kind of information to better support a feature team.

Planning and Tracking Tools

The basis for all tracking during an iteration is the iteration plan. As previously stated, post an iteration plan prominently and ensure its accessibility, allowing every team member to both read and edit it. Collocated teams can use a project poster or planning wall on which to affix index cards, moving the cards as feature status progresses from to-do to done-done to delivered. There are commercial tools that mimic this behavior and that distributed teams might find helpful. My projects usually are quite happy with open-source tools, not only because they are free, but also because they do not unnecessarily increase complexity.

The tool that I consider to be the best performer is Trac.[18] One of the reasons it works well for distributed projects is that it is simple, easy to use, and easy to customize. Features such as a link to Subversion allow connecting a successful integration into the system with moving the task into the done-done state.[19] We also employ a wiki that's integrated in Trac (so we do not need a separate tool for our communication platform). We also use the in Trac integrated blog facility to record impediments stated at the daily synchronization, making sure only to capture those impediments of interest to multiple teams and that need special attention. We use Trac both for long-term planning and for iteration planning and tracking.

No matter what tools a team uses, it must ensure the following:

- *Everyone can easily access tools:* Integrate iteration planning and tracking tools with the development environment so it is always open on everybody's desktop.

---

[18] For Trac, see http://trac.edgewall.org/, also Agile-Trac: http://www.agile-trac.org.

[19] For Subversion, see http://subversion.tigris.org/.

- *The team's progress is made transparent:* The tool should visually represent development progress by, for instance, ordering or color-coding the tasks for quick recognition.
- *Every team member can read and edit with the tools:* To maintain relevant tracking information, everyone should be able to update the iteration plan at any time. If a tool is difficult to use (for instance, it requires a special environment or licenses), team members can't use it.

Search for a tool that meets your team's needs. The open-source tools XPlanner and PPTS as well as many commercial tools provide a wide variety of planning options.[20] The best tool is the one you use over and again, and never collects dust.

Keeping Goals in Focus

Tracking iteration progress helps to visualize useful data during an iteration:

- *Focus on highest-priority features:* A team should focus on high-priority features (those that yield the highest business value) first and avoid starting tasks related to lower-priority features in parallel. In case a team runs out of time, this strategy will prevent it having started work on all features but delivering none.
- *Define remaining work:* As Scrum suggests, I always ask team members to re-estimate at the end of the day how much time they will need to finish all tasks they have started working on. It is unimportant, however, to know how much time someone has already spent working on a specific task. Likewise, it is not a means to check if initial estimates turn out to be correct. The point of re-estimation is to know if the remaining tasks team members can finish during the remainder of the iteration.
- *Measure progress:* On many of my projects, we subdivide the status of specific tasks to show if they are to-do, in-progress, to-be-verified, or done-done. The initial state of a task (after planning) is the to-do state. As soon as somebody starts working on it, it moves into the in-progress state. Once a task is in progress, ask the team member

---

20For XPlanner, see http://xplanner.org/. For PPTS, see http://ses-ppts.sourceforge.net.

responsible for it to re-estimate the remaining effort at the end of the day, unless the task is finished. After the developer has finished the task (designed, implemented, tested, and integrated), it moves into the to-be-verified state. In order to reach the final done-done state, the task has to be verified. (Verification depends on the task—sometimes it could mean that this task finalizes a feature thus the end-to-end acceptance test has to be run maybe even in a different environment, or somebody needs to review it, or that an automatic check ensures it meets certain requirements.)

Individual team members complete all of these tracking activities. It might be necessary that the coach reminds them from time to time. The information gathered should be relevant to everyone interested in the project. Thus it is helpful if different information related to the different states of a task, for example, can be color-coded or otherwise visually organized.

Naturally, if the big-picture visual scheme signals trouble, team members know to look into the details to resolve problems.

Keeping Goals in Focus

7.5 Dealing With Change

If the product owner realizes that some originally planned features have become obsolete, or that priorities have completely changed, iterations allow him or her to take these changes into account. Each feature team plans to deliver several features in an iteration. If a change happens, this change can be taken into account when planning the next iteration. The Agile Manifesto reminds us that change, rather than a cause for despair, presents opportunity: "Welcome changing requirements, even late in development. Agile processes harness change for the customer's competitive advantage."[21]

Each feature team has the full responsibility for their features. This reduces the additional effort for coordination and integration compared to sub-teams being structured instead according

---

[21] Agile Manifesto online: http://agilemanifesto.org/principles.html.

to technical components. In the latter setting the responsibility for completing a feature including the required changes, would be distributed over several sub-teams and would have to be organized accordingly.

Iteration Length Marks Response Time

Agile projects address all changes including, of course, feature priority and content, during iteration-planning meetings. Thus, the shorter the iteration length, the easier is it to integrate changes because of quicker response to changing requirements. If a team strives for better response time to customer change, to cut down on interrupting iterations (which shouldn't happen anyway), consider shortening iteration length to decrease response time.

Keep in mind that iterations should be long enough for developers to deliver several features per feature team. On some projects, we schedule one-week long iterations that allow a great response time to changes, as well as high-speed feature delivery. Two-week iterations are typical, and prove many times over to be an adequate length on large distributed projects. You will have to come up with an iteration length that works for you, but you will have to reconsider the length if a shorter response time to change is requested.

Change-Request Scheduling

Treat a change request the same way as any other feature. The product owner must prioritize an approved change request to incorporate it and plan its development during a later iteration. Processing change requests grows more complicated if a feature team works on a new release of a product while at the same time maintaining an earlier release of the same product that's already in production. If such a team works for instance in two-week iterations, the response time for deploying the change request for the release in production is maximum four weeks – if the change request was made at the very beginning of the current iteration– but most often the response time is much shorter, because the change request has been made later during the actual iteration. Thus most often the iteration length is short enough so that the response time of the feature team is quick enough. If this is not the case, first of all you should consider to shorten the iteration length.

If iteration length is only one week, it is very difficult to shorten it. I recommend including a buffer for ad-hoc change requests in the iteration plan. This buffer is limited, for example by a two-day time-box or five complexity points. Whenever my teams need such a buffer, we assign it the highest priority within the iteration: Whenever a change request comes in, and we have not already used the buffer, the change request is our highest priority. Whoever is available works on the change request. As soon as a feature team has used the buffer in the actual iteration, it refuses additional ad-hoc change requests. We limit the buffer to avoid the risk of a team not further progressing with the new release of the product due to the permanent work on change requests.

Team-Structure Change

In contrast to feature-driven development, to ensure utmost feature-team effectiveness through team identity, I normally try to keep feature-team members together during the lifetime of a project. Future projects also benefit from keeping together successful teams. A substantial change, however, might require that a feature team reorganizes (for example, if some functionality changes completely). On one of my projects, we had to restructure some feature teams completely, because the specific domain these teams had focused on had been deleted from the project's scope entirely.

Continual disruption due to frequent team restructuring is problematic. Never overlook the price restructuring exacts. It always takes some time before a new team really works together as a team. For this reason, I always try to bring a whole feature team together at one site after restructuring it, the same way as at the beginning of the project. Travel expenses (depending on the degree of team distribution) are offset by improved team effectiveness.

If you are unsure of the benefit of an in-person meeting, visualize the effect of the duration of the team's calibration for better traceability. Every agile project employs many different metrics. When changing a team structure, determine the impact on, for example, a team's velocity. For example, extremely growing a team is typically reflected by a thirty percent drop in the team's velocity. Visualizing these effects will help arguing for the necessary actions.

7.6 Overall Project Plan

The product owner or owners steer feature development through iterations. But in order to know if a project will complete all promised deliverables by its deadline, develop an overall project plan. As Highsmith notes, a project plan should enable a team, not confine it: "Agile projects are not controlled by conformance to plan but by conformance to business value. ...If we accept the notion of constant change and turbulence, then plans are still useful as guides, but not as control mechanisms—because they tend to punish correct actions."[22] Understand that this is not an artifact but a vivified document that will change and develop.

Release Planning

It is not only easier to steer a project if features are packaged into meaningful releases (from the business perspective), but doing so also solicits useful feedback, and can even lead to an early market debut. Such kinds of clusters of features are sometimes called feature packs. Whereas a single feature is intended to provide business value for a customer, a feature pack might enable the customer to begin using a version of a working system. Even if a team does not plan to go into production when completing a specific feature pack, it can use the practice opportunity to obtain better feedback. It is always easier to provide comprehensive, meaningful tests if they investigate not only the functional or technical aspects of a system but also user experience.

Many projects term the completion of a feature pack a release. Sometimes we differentiate between an internal release and an external release, which will ship to the customer as a finished product. An external release means that the system will in fact go into production whereas an internal release will go through each single step an external release does except for the final step into production. Structure the overall project plan to include several internal or external releases or a combination of both, depending on the customer's needs.

---

[22]J.A. Highsmith, op. cit., p. 32.

It is the responsibility of the product owner(s) to define meaningful feature packs based on customers' and other stakeholders' interests. The product owner(s) also decide release delivery dates. Coaches, with help from their teams, then verify this release plan. They will cross-check when the team can deliver releases, depending on team velocity. Architects validate that feature-team assignments are not interdependent. If they uncover dependencies, they will create a lookahead plan to reassign or minimize dependencies.

Forecasting

At the very beginning of the project the first iteration plan will be used to forecast the remaining project. By planning your first iteration you will have assumed a velocity (because you don't know the actual velocity, yet). Now for verifying the deliveries, you can compute how many iterations you have available for each (internal or external) release; because the dates for the releases are determined from the business side (product owner or rather the customer) and the length of the iteration has defined as well. Imagine it's now beginning of March and your next release is determined for the beginning of June and your iterations last two weeks –therefore you will have six iterations available for finishing the release. You can apply this to all further releases as well. For each iteration you can assume the same velocity as you've assumed for the first iteration. For instance, if your assumed velocity is 20 points for the first iteration, you can verify how many features you will be able to deliver in your next release. Applying this to each of the planned releases, enables you to come up with a release plan.

Please note that especially the first version of your release plan will probably not be accurate, because the velocity for the iterations is only assumed but not proven. Therefore, if you have a different (working) technique in place for coming up with a first release plan – I see no problem in using that one, yet you still need to ensure that the release plan will be improved with every iteration. Not the first release plan is key, but the better precision you will gain with every iteration. Only this will allow you to know exactly what you can deliver at any given point in time.

Most often you will plan your first iteration with one (collocated) team only. Therefore, in a distributed setting you need to make according adjustments to the above suggested forecast. In most of the projects you will have an idea about the timing and up-scaling of the project. So you are aware of when will the whole team will both grow and spread and by which degree. Your best guess for the moment is to assume that all future teams will have the same velocity as your first team. You might furthermore consider following a suggestion from Scrum[23] and add the following drag factor: 1.2 because you will work in a distributed setting and additionally 0.4 because you have multiple teams working on the same product. This drag factor will decrease your assumed velocity – you can either multiply the estimates with the drag factor and keep the same velocity, or divide the velocity by the drag factor. So for instance if you follow the latter advice, if your assumed velocity was twenty, then taking the above drag factor into account means that you should calculate only with a velocity of 12.5 from the time you will have multiple teams spread globally working on the project. Yet, I would recommend to use the assumed velocity for you first iteration for all future teams as a starting point, although this will very unlikely be accurate. However, all other guesses (as well considering the drag factor) won't be any more precise at this point in time. The real power comes with the iterations, only they will help you to improve your plan over time.

Release versus Milestone

Although a release marks a milestone, the two are distinct: A release is time-boxed, with a fixed release date. A milestone, although promised for a specific date but it is only bound to the accomplishment of some pre-defined functionality. Although feature teams and customers generally agree to the feature packs included in a release, the specific contents are not fixed, leaving slack for a feature team to react to unforeseen events (new requirements, fluctuating velocity, technical problems, or priority changes, for example). The team as a whole stands by its promise to deliver a system consisting of valuable features selected by the customer that work by a fixed date.

Many agile teams prefer promising a release date to promising pre-defined functionality because requirements and priorities change, often enabling the team to develop a better market

---

[23] Scrum provides this information in its course. Or you can find this as well on the web at: http://www.controlchaos.com/module/practicing_pelrine.pdf

advantage. A team might postpone milestones to capitalize on changes. Postponing milestones, however, doesn't help build a trusting relationship with a customer.

The overall project plan (sometimes called the release plan) tracks the big picture of a project. Neither release dates nor feature packs should surprise anyone working on the project, no matter the location. The overall project plan is making the common vision transparent for everyone on even a widely distributed team.

7.7 Summary

Steering an iteration through features helps to keep the focus on the delivery of the business value While some people believe that agile development is an unplanned (maybe even chaotic) approach, the opposite is true. An agile teams always reflect actual project status as well as changes made throughout development. The difference between many traditional teams and an agile team is that for an agile team, a plan is not an artifact but is instead an activity. Agility is an appropriate approach for global software development. As Biehl concludes, "Detailed planning, flexibility during implementation, and competent leadership are much more crucial for implementing a global IS than for implementing a local IS."[24]

Planning Poker is a great way for feature-team members to gain not only a better understanding about required features but also to estimate those features. When every team on a project conducts its own Planning Poker sessions, it will be necessary to periodically re-calibrate the estimation baseline. The greatest advantage is that each feature team will assume ownership of its own estimates and, more importantly, willlearn about features it will develop.

A team should also track its development iterations to ensure delivery every time. Individual teams are best positioned to monitor velocity and to respond quickly to risks that threaten completion of iteration goals. Designing and keeping up-to-date an overall project plan helps teams prevent losing sight of their project goals. Flesh out project-plan details for upcoming iter-

---

[24]M. Biehl, op. cit., p. 58.

ations with a lookahead plan if dependencies between feature teams threaten development.

8. Eliciting Feedback and Conducting Retrospectives

Learning without thought is labor lost;
thought without learning is perilous.

— Confucius

Agility is about quick feedback loops, not only involving the customer but also a whole project team. Gather feedback to reduce the risk of aiming for the wrong objectives, especially focusing on the following three areas:

- *The system*
    - How well does system integration work across different sites and teams?
    - How does overall quality look during and following unit, integration, system, and acceptance testing?
- *The progress*
    - Are we developing the right product?
    - Is the customer happy with the system under development?
    - Do we manage to deliver what we promise?
- *The process*
    - Does the development process support us?
    - Is the support of the process adequate?
    - What needs to change to improve efficiency?
    - What "best practices" should we spread so all teams benefit?

Quick feedback loops present their own challenges. First, the project team must enable every members to provide and obtain feedback about the whole system, the process, and tools. Second, the team must connect to the customer. Selecting a product owner to act as a customer representative at each site helps ensure that a team develops features of the highest business value.

8.1 Customer Feedback

As has been frequently noted, a primary goal of agile projects is to deliver software products or entire systems that completely satisfy and delight the customer. Therefore, the product owner, as a member of the team, ensures the focus on the highest business value. In rare cases, the product owner is a customer himself, but even then he won't be the only user of the system.

For providing a successful product, we need to obtain and incorporate the feedback from all the different customers. The product owner is the major connection to the different customers. He enables the customers being aware of the actual status of the project, to try out the system, and to provide feedback. The product owner has to balance the different opinions of the customers and make decisions regarding further development activities.

Identifying the Customer

Identifying the real customer can be quite difficult, especially so because there are different kinds of customers to take into account. Additionally, not all customers are external to a project's domain and sometimes they even may be another group of developers who will take a project's output to embed in its own product or system to satisfy a different customer. For instance, on one project we were developing a tool for a different group of developers who provided some software for cars. At first my team considered the car drivers instead of this other group of developers as end user. The real customer, then, is whatever person or group can provide the most-useful feedback regarding the product or system being built.

Typically, stakeholders are the most visible of customers because they usually control the project's budget and they generally pay for product development. However, it is essential that projects not overlook another interest group: the end users. End users are critically important to a project's development effort because they provide the most-valuable feedback.

To establish a solid channel of communication with end users on one of my projects, we sent a small group of developers and business analysts to the end user's site so that project members could observe the customer performing daily work. We used the on-site opportunity to get to know the customer but also to discuss features we had not yet developed, thereby confirming that our understanding of desired system functionality was complete. On another project, we invited end-users to our site to work with the system under development. Offering customers different opportunities to evaluate development progress should improve both the quality of the final product and overall customer satisfaction.

Distant Customer

The team relies most of the time on the product owners' feedback. Yet, for avoiding the risk of the product owner overlooking important customer issues or even more important for discovering the possibility of having the wrong product owner (as it happened in one of my projects), the team needs from time to time direct customer feedback. Especially in a distributed environment very often the customer is not located next door. For still obtaining regular feedback on the real system, you have to make the system available to the customer. For example, allow the customer to download the system at the end of every iteration via the inter- or intranet.

For establishing and preserving a good relationship between the project and the customer, we often invite the customer to the iteration review (if the distance allows this) or at least to the release iteration review. If this is impossible, we enable the participation of the customer in the review meeting via virtual communication facilities.

In one of my projects we didn't succeed with our invitations to the customer. The customer just didn't show up. Although we had good product owners being able to stay in touch with the customers, we still decided that we all prefer to obtain direct customer feedback at least occasionally. Thus, we had some people representing the whole project actually traveling to the customer site and present the newly built system there.

Customer Presentations

A way projects may obtain extremely valuable feedback is to invite customers to demo a deliverable—even a newly built system—to show the whole team how well what it has built works. For this approach to succeed, team members must give customers time to play and familiarize themselves with the new deliverable in advance of their presentation. Giving customers the opportunity to show developers how they use deliverables benefits both parties:

- Customers begin to identify more closely with the project, becoming part of a whole team of people who are pulling together to accomplish a common, defined goal.
- Developers learn about how customers want to use the deliverable or system, gaining perspective beyond a specific section of the system into how the big picture is shaping up.

Inviting customers to present at the end of every iteration is probably not doable for the customer and also impractical on most distributed global projects. Most likely, not every feature team would benefit from the frequent customer's visit anyway, because they are located at a different site. But it can be quite feasible to schedule presentations for release iterations— or for instance, at the end of every third or fourth iteration— and establish a rhythm to enhance contact among the whole development team and the customers.

8.2 Review Meetings

At the end of a development cycle –an iteration or a release– the team looks at the achievements. We try to meet in person for the review meetings. If impossible we run the meeting using diverse communication tools for making the virtual meetings effective. Even then, we try to meet in person at least every eight to twelve weeks. Schedule all in-person meetings to match a rhythm in sync with development iterations or releases, not according to an arbitrary calendar period.

Iteration Reviews

Most often, agile projects schedule the iteration review back-to-back with the following iteration's planning meeting. Conduct iteration reviews to recall the commitment for the past iteration and analyze actual, developed features. The feature team presents its deliveries and comments on the achievements. The product owner concludes the presentation by taking (again) a stand on the accepted and rejected features.

Finally, the feature team -ensured by the coach- will compute its velocity. This newly computed velocity will be used as an input for the next planning meeting. This allows the team's commitment or rather the realization of the iteration plan to improve with every iteration. The updated velocity of each feature team will be summed up to the project's velocity. This more accurate project velocity will then be used to update the overall project plan. This way the overall project plan is getting more precise with every iteration.

The feature-team presentation to the product owner should not bring anything to light that is a surprise. Since the developers regularly communicate with their product owner about advances and obstacles, the presentation serves as a jumping-off point for analysis of the product. For example, information communicated at the daily synchronization sessions should alert everyone involved as to what to expect at the end of the iteration. If anyone truly is surprised, this should be regarded as a smell that the parties have not been communicating effectively, and shows that they need to find ways to improve.

Review Meetings – Dispersed Individually versus In-Person Jointly

The review meeting has its main purpose in closing a development cycle -an iteration or review- it can serve as well for re-establishing a joint understanding of the big picture across all teams. Depending on the size of a project and its degree of distribution, schedule all teams to meet together periodically, according to the following recommendations:

- For forty project members distributed across, say, several European countries, I recommend bringing all forty people together at the end of every other iteration and changing the site for each meeting.
- For forty project members perhaps spread throughout the United States, India, and Europe, I recommend bringing all forty together only after every third or fourth iteration, again at changing sites.

- For one hundred project members spread all around the globe, I recommend selecting representatives from every team, including from the host-site team, to meet at changing sites after every third or fourth iteration.

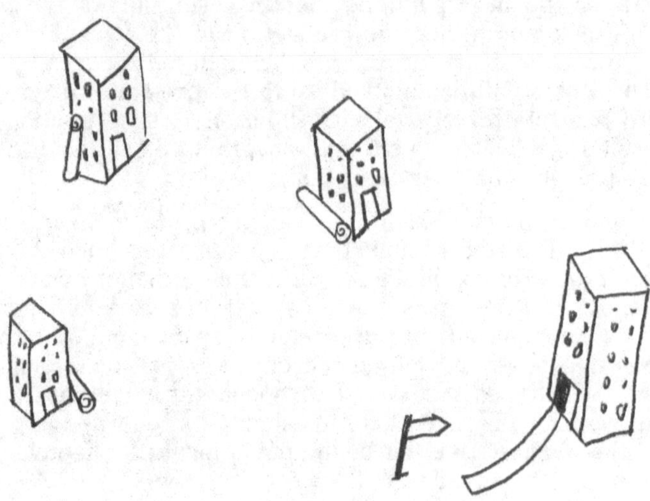

Changing Sites

If the iteration review is a project-wide meeting, then the ritual of stating the previous commitments, presenting the deliveries and evaluating the outcome is done feature team after feature team. Care has to be taken, that every feature team has a pre-defined time-box to review its achievements, to keep the length of the meeting under control. It is important that members from all feature teams get the idea of the big picture of the system under development. However some details might not be too interesting for members belonging to a different feature team than the one presenting. For project members not being present at this meeting we enable their participation via a web cam or video recording.

Consider travel practicality when conducting individual feature-team review meetings. If a feature team is dispersed, the best option is for all members of the team to meet during every iteration at changing sites. If some team members are located far from the rest of the team, they can participate in review meetings via videoconferencing or virtual-meeting facilities. Consider as well the difficulty of coordinating people in different time zones. My recommendation is to change the time for the virtual review meetings so that it is comfortable at least at one point in time for every team member.

Sometimes, a product owner steers several feature teams. If the product owner is responsible for several collocated feature teams, members easily can meet in one room. If one product owner steers several feature teams that are not located at the same site, the strategy should be the same as for the dispersed feature team. So either bring together at changing sites all feature teams for which he or she is responsible or use virtual meeting facilities. Most typically, the reason a product owner steers several feature teams is that those teams all focus on a similar domain area in the system and are developing related features. They should conduct review and planning meetings together or at least side by side.

Release Reviews

Three to six iterations typically make up a release. For the release review I always try to bring everyone—if project size allows—together face-to-face. If this is impractical, I limit the get-together to, for instance, two (changing) representatives per feature team. Other members can connect to this meeting virtually.

The release review is quite similar to the iteration review: Members recall initial commitments and present deliverables; the product owners comment on accepted or rejected features; and the whole team analyzes the velocity. The difference is that the scope of a release review covers not just the past iteration, but also the past release (three to six iterations). Because of the wider scope of a release review, it is essential either that the whole project meet or that every feature team sends representatives to the meeting.

8.3 Retrospectives

Unlike the review meeting which serves for analyzing the result produced over a defined timeframe, the retrospective helps examining the usefulness of the development approach. [1] Only if you include retrospectives you will follow an agile approach. This reasoning is born of the first value comparison and last principle in the Agile Manifesto: "Individuals and interactions over processes and tools . . . At regular intervals, the team reflects on how to become more effective, then tunes and adjusts its behavior accordingly."[2]

I interpret the first value statement to mean that we must ensure that every agile process serves individuals and their interactions. The second statement mandates regular reflection sessions—that is, retrospectives. Retrospectives are a means to establish and preserve the agile value system by allowing teams to shape the development process to best support their work.

A retrospective is a session for reflection and analysis that in traditional projects usually generates some documentation by the project manager, but it is its function as a regularly scheduled, ongoing, evaluation and planning tool owned by the whole team that is of interest in agile development. Sometimes called lessons-learned or post-mortem sessions, retrospectives frequently are only conducted at the end of a failed project, when all project members meet for the last time to reflect on how to avoid similar failure in the future and what to do differently next time. To practice agility, retrospectives must be conducted regularly throughout development. Highsmith notes, "We have to test our knowledge constantly—using practices like retrospectives. These should be done after each iterative cycle rather than waiting until the end of the project. The quality of learning derived from this practice shows an organization's true commitment to learning, and therefore, a key to its adaptability."[3]

Although team members can learn by waiting to conduct a retrospective at a project's end, they miss out on opportunities to shape the development process and make use of lessons learned while still working on the project. Consequently, in addition to performing a summary retrospective at the end of a project, agile projects align periodic retrospectives with

---

[1] For a thorough treatment of the topic, see N.L. Kerth, *Project Retrospectives: A Handbook for Team Reviews* (New York: Dorset House Publishing, 2001).

[2] Agile Manifesto online, see: http://agilemanifesto.org.

[3] J.A. Highsmith, III, "Project Management at the Edge," *The IT Project Leader* (February 2000), p. 2. Also available online: http://www.jimhighsmith.com/pubs.html/PMEdge.pdf.

the heartbeat of project iterations (hence the terms *iteration retrospective* and *heartbeat retrospective)*.

Before delving into the specifics of how to conduct retrospectives in a global setting, let's see what retrospectives intend to accomplish. Of primary importance as noted by Kerth, a retrospective is "not an activity of finding fault with anyone, but rather an activity for learning from experiences."[4]

A retrospective is a call to team members to reflect on project development thus far, asking them to individually evaluate past events, which have built the joint history of the team. Team members are called upon to examine this historical data to identify practices that worked well and those to improve. Based on its inspection of events and data, the team builds an action plan to implement change for the remainder of the project.

If a project is to shape ongoing development processes on the basis of what is learned in a retrospective, team members first need to classify types of processes in use. On large global projects, I identify at least two different types:

- *Individual-feature-team process:* Feature teams, sooner or later, develop customized conventions and guidelines. Although everyone can benefit from the findings of one team, not all conventions are meaningful for other feature teams.[5] To enable every feature team to improve most effectively, team members must recognize that no two feature teams follow exactly the same process.
- *Project-wide process:* Work involving diverse feature teams calls for a common set of guidelines to define the development process. Examples are performing integration and build, or the iteration length and turnover day – these are things that have an impact on every feature team.

If your project is small (for instance, comprising fewer than thirty team members), and not widely distributed, try to always bring the whole project together for reviews, retrospectives, and planning meetings. Split into subgroups dealing with individual-feature-team issues and then re-group to discuss joint, project-wide processes.

---

[4]N.L. Kerth, op. cit., p. 85.

[5]For more information about establishing a common development culture, see Chapter 9, "Customizing Practices."

Individual-Feature-Team Retrospectives

All members of one feature team should meet together in one room. If team members are dispersed, schedule rotating meeting locations or meet with everyone virtually. On all my projects, we schedule a retrospective right after review meetings, utilizing the same organizational techniques. Scheduling a retrospective after a review meeting not only makes sense logistically but is also most productive and relevant. After reviewing the past iteration in the review meeting, look at the reasons behind the project's progression. Discussion of achievements leads nicely into the retrospective.

While discussing what worked and what didn't and more important what needs to be improved, how, by whom and till when, a feature team might discover certain successes or failures that can not be adjusted by the individual feature team, but instead only by the community of all the feature teams. Conduct individual-feature-team retrospectives before those involving the whole project.

Project-Wide Retrospectives

The project-wide retrospective is a means to improve the inter-working of feature teams. All feature teams will report their findings in their individual feature team retrospectives by focusing on things that are of interest for the other feature teams. These findings will be used as an input for improving the process across all feature teams. Depending on the size of a project, consider limiting participants to several representatives from each feature team.

Schedule project-wide retrospectives depending on the feature teams' satisfaction and general progress. Often, my projects bind a project-wide retrospective with a project-wide review meeting. Additionally, we have found that face-to-face retrospectives prove to be much more productive than a virtual retrospective, and that, if the process is in fairly good shape, scheduling project-wide retrospectives only for every third iteration or after every (internal or external) release can suffice. However, if our development process is not in good shape (possibly true at the beginning of a project or after bringing more people aboard), we schedule a project-wide retrospective at the end of every iteration. Only every third retrospective need be in-person, but analyzing progress more frequently will allow team members to realign project trajectory.

If the project-wide retrospective is an in-person meeting with two or so representatives from each feature team, plan communication channels to connect them to their respective individual-feature-team retrospectives. Three approaches that facilitate this connection follow:

- *Schedule an individual-feature-team retrospective before reps attend a project-wide retrospective.* This approach can succeed but a disadvantage is that the current iteration will decrease by at least one day, depending on members' travel time to the project-wide retrospective. The feature teams could alternatively conduct the iteration planning and start the iteration without the representatives. Unfortunately the actions decided in the project-wide retrospective can not be considered during planning following this strategy. Most often, it is only practical for the feature team(s) located at the project-wide retrospective host site to pursue this approach.
- *Conduct individual-feature-team retrospectives virtually.* Feature teams send reps to the project-wide retrospective and otherwise conduct individual retrospectives normally, connecting traveling representatives virtually. (Some dispersed feature teams always conduct meetings virtually.)
- *Conduct individual-feature-team retrospectives without the participation of project-wide retrospective reps.* The advantage here is that no special communication channel or scheduling complicates the meeting. The major disadvantage is that project-wide retrospective representatives are not involved—and they are responsible for providing the results of the feature-team retrospective to the project-wide retrospective. Most often, collocated feature teams that are not located at the project-wide retrospective site usually prefer this approach.

Although none of these approaches is ideal, they are all acceptable in certain circumstances. For smaller project teams (e.g. including approximate three feature teams) all project members and not only the representatives take part in the project-wide retrospective. In such a setting, we alternate between individual feature team retrospectives and project-wide retrospectives. The point is for team members, feature teams, and entire projects to communicate with one another about retrospective findings.

Joint-Site Retrospectives

It is helpful also to conduct joint-site retrospectives—all project members (independent of affiliation to a feature team) working at one project site. I recommend substituting a joint-site retrospective for either individual-feature-team or project-wide team retrospectives from time to time to focus on site-specific practices and issues. Share the results of the joint-site retrospective at project-wide meetings or in the project's wiki if such findings are more widely applicable.

Retrospective Protocol

Following discussion of retrospective participants and groupings, let's now look more closely at procedures. First off, no matter what type of retrospective, it is a coach's responsibility to conduct it. This doesn't necessarily mean that the coach facilitates the session, just that the coach organizes the retrospective, ensuring that meeting facilities are reserved for the group and ensuring that a qualified facilitator will run it. Most of the time, a coach will actually facilitate; however, on some of my teams, the product owner or a regular team member as volunteer moderator conducts the meeting.

In some cases, it might be necessary to recruit a facilitator from outside the team, the project, or even the organization (for instance, if team members are not getting along or if for any other reasons an objective facilitator is required). If no one has experience conducting a retrospective, consider recruiting an external facilitator at the beginning of the project so that team members can learn proper protocol from an expert.

Virtual Retrospectives

To conduct a retrospective virtually, I highly recommend distributing a survey in advance to identify the most pressing topics. Team members should complete and return this survey anonymously. Then, use survey results to create an agenda for the retrospective.[6]

---

[6]Thanks to Ainsley Nies for sharing this facilitation technique.

The survey can also jump-start a retrospective. For example, I participated on several large, virtual retrospectives, for which everyone answered classic retrospective questions such as the following in advance:

- *What has worked well that we should remember and continue?*
- *What should we do differently?*
- *What continues to puzzle us?*

Thinking about such questions beforehand helps participants keep retrospectives focused, as well as prevents unnecessarily prolonged meetings. Maintaining participants' engagement during virtual meetings is even more difficult than when face-to-face. Time-box a retrospective in advance, depending on the timeframe you're looking at, on the familiarity with the process, the frequency of the retrospectives and on the amount of participants. Even with the best facilitation techniques, it is difficult to conduct productive virtual meetings longer than one hour. Consider splitting the retrospective and focusing on the reflection in the first session and the prioritization and action planning in the second session. However, this leaves the first session very open at the end and might keep people from coming back to the second –more important– session.

Especially for release and end-of-project retrospectives, one hour is too short to hear every voice. Briefly extend retrospectives, after a break, or plan additional meetings to address specific topics.

A retrospective has always the idea to give every participant a voice. This can be more difficult when conducting a global retrospective virtually. Speaking out loud over the phone and in a foreign language is not for everyone. Strategies like round robin help participants to speak up and as well quiets the extroverts.

Distributed Retrospectives by Linda Rising[a]

You'll find a lot of agreement among those who study the successes and failures of distributed teams that having as much contact and communication as possible among team members increases the likelihood of success. It seems obvious. Of course face-to-face trumps remote interaction. Of course sending representatives back and forth is invaluable. But what can you do within the distributed environment? What can team members do if travel is not an option or if travel is limited, so that most of the project effort is spent working within a distributed setting, and the retrospective must be a virtual meeting? Here's one dialogue reporting a successful distributed retrospective.

> *"Thanks to all of you for taking the time to share your points of view on our project. I'd like to remind you to put your phones on mute so we can all hear each other better. Please speak slowly and clearly and identify yourself before you comment. I hope you remembered to bring three lists with you that you created in thinking back over the project. You were looking for answers to the following questions: One: What worked well that we should continue on the next release? Two: What should be done differently? Three: What still puzzles you?*
>
> *"I'm going to ask for the answers to each question, starting with 'What worked well?' and I'd like to use a round-robin format. Please just contribute one of your answers or say 'Pass' if you have nothing more to add. Let's use this order: Charlie, Lucy, Snoopy, Sally, Patty, Marcie. I'll call your name, so you won't need to identify yourself for this part of the session.*
>
> *"We should all remember that we have agreed to follow The Prime Directive. It's good to mention names for appreciation, but not for blaming. Remember, we are here to learn. Before we begin, are there any questions?"*
>
> *"Hi, this is Lucy. What if someone gives an answer we had on our list?"*
>
> *"Good question. I'm going to suggest that we use a protocol from the writers' workshop process used in the patterns community[b]. If someone says something you agree with, un-mute your phone and just say, 'Gush.' We won't count the gushes but Schroeder, our scribe, will note that the comment had support from others. Other questions?"*

The retrospective proceeded for about an hour-and-a-half and produced many comments and suggestions.

> *"Other comments or suggestions before we close this part of the retrospective? Then I'd like to close the session by having the team members offer appreciations. You remember that anyone can appreciate anyone else on the team, even someone who isn't on the call. Who would like to go first?"*

The offer-appreciations exercise is an effective way to bring a team together, whether distributed or face-to-face.

After the call, the notes were sent around to the group for prioritization. During this round of e-mail, a few other comments and suggestions were added. The results were handed over to the team working on the next release.

It is possible to do an effective distributed retrospective and enable group learning. No magic involved! Kerth's Prime Directive states, "Regardless of what we discover, we must understand and truly believe that everyone did the best job he or she could, given what was known at the time, his or her skills and abilities, the resources available, and the situation at hand."[c] The Prime Directive is an operational value that solicits useful results from a retrospective. It changes participants' focus from blame to learning. Over time, it can permeate all team interactions and efforts.

[a]Linda Rising (USA), independent consultant, www.lindarising.org

[b]Richard P. Gabriel. Writers' Workshop and the Work of Making Things. Addison-Wesley. 2002

[c]N.L. Kerth, op. cit., p. 7.

Attendees

It should be obvious that all members of a feature team – including the product owner– will participate in the individual-feature-team retrospective. As discussed earlier, depending on the project's size (changing) representatives of each feature team will participate in the project-wide retrospective. For joint site retrospectives every project member who resides at this site should participate in this retrospective, independent if he belongs to a feature team or not.

We invite additionally people who belong as well to the project but not necessarily to a specific feature team, examples are the project manager, or –more important– the customer. Especially if the retrospective is scheduled after finishing a release it is very helpful to have the customer (and not only the lead product owner) present. As Ainsley Nies experienced: "When the customer is not the product owner, I think there are times when including the customer can add a lot of value – like release retrospectives. [...] It also can bring out any communication issues between the PO [product owner] and customer that wouldn't otherwise be apparent." [7]

Common Retrospective Mistakes

- *The desire to make the whole world a better place:* Especially during their first retrospective, team members have many great ideas about how to improve the process or the situation in the project. It is very important to acknowledge and record those ideas (for instance recording the ideas on the wiki)—but it is even more important to refrain from trying to change everything at once. Discuss early that you will pursue change in a gradual, iterative manner, thereby preventing team members from becoming frustrated by their perceived inability to make a difference. Focus on only one to three issues and come up with a realistic action plan. Take one change at a time is for some teams the only possibility to adapt and sustain change.
- *No hands on deck:* Often, people assume that once their team discusses an issue, the world will change all by itself. Publish an action plan that shows who will do what, when, with the help of whom. It might be necessary to take those actions into account in the next planning meeting, because they will not only require some action but as well some time from team members. Then, track actions and completion of tasks (for example, in the daily synchronization).
- *Change is the norm:* To successfully implement successive change, acknowledge the progress already made. Begin a retrospective by looking at the outcome (the action plan)

---

[7] Ainsley Nies. Private conversation.

of the previous retrospective and celebrate the success of implemented change. If some of the planned actions have not been executed successfully, treat this as input for the current retrospective before tackling other changes.

Facilitation Techniques

Facilitation Techniques

The frequency of retrospectives can cause boredom, especially if a team uses the same facilitation techniques for every retrospective. In addition to changing facilitators, also change moderation techniques.[8]

Although on most of my projects team members appreciate a variety of facilitation techniques, some consistency helps build a safe environment. On one project, I led a feature-team retrospective with four related feature teams. I used a metaplan technique during the first few retrospectives.[9] To establish the process of retrospectives, I use the same facilitation techniques until participants grow used to the approach. After we develop several iterations, and therefore conduct several retrospectives, I change facilitation techniques in an attempt to maintain interest in the retrospective. At the end of one

---

[8]For a useful set of facilitation techniques for conducting retrospectives, see E. Derby and D. Larsen, *Agile Retrospectives: Making Good Teams Great* (Raleigh, N.C.: Pragmatic Programmer, 2006).

[9]For my description of the metaplan technique for retrospectives, see Eckstein, op. cit., pp. 106-7.

particular retrospective, I presented a short reflection on the retrospective itself and was astonished to hear that all team members wanted "their" metaplan technique back. For this team, the facilitation technique itself had turned into ritual: The technique kept people grounded in their changing world and helped them to focus on the lessons learned in the past iteration.

Facilitating an Effective Virtual Retrospective by Debra Lavell[a]

A significant part of the work I do at Intel is to engage with key product-development teams to improve their software development practices. Such process improvement efforts are always a challenge, especially if you are tasked to look at all the activities to deliver finished end-user software products, out-of-box solutions, or a combination of sub-processes. The problems are compounded when dealing with geographically dispersed teams, cultural differences, and disparate time zones with few overlapping work hours.

At Intel, very few software teams are located in the same country, same state, much less in the same building. We have teams spread out among approximately 290 locations in over 45 countries. One way we have approached teams asking for help to improve their software processes is to conduct a retrospective. At Intel, we describe a retrospective as a ritual where:

- The team reflects periodically, we have identified three strategic points across the software development life cycle (so teams can apply lessons learned and continuously improve).
- The retrospective is led by a trained, objective facilitator, who follows a defined, objective process.
- We use this time as an opportunity for the team to focus on the learnings to improve in a constructive way.
- The goal is to guide the team and any subsequent teams to actionable change in the form of action plans (improved effectiveness and efficiency).
- The outputs yield results via one or two key improvements implemented by the team's commitment to change.

How do you facilitate an *effective* retrospective in spite

of all the global challenges? Our solution: We do a virtual retrospective. Here are few tricks we have found to help:

Gather participants into a few locations:

- Try to have as many participants congregate in as few locations as possible. Reserve *conference rooms at strategic locations* for participants to assemble, equipped with collaboration devices such as an Infocus-type projection system to attach to a computer to display in each room. The objective is to create synergy with those in each room and then use activities to cross-pollinate ideas to collectively decide on a course of action.
- Designate a *facilitator for each location*, and poll locations regularly for questions and input. Use online instant messaging (IM) or other ichat software to help conduct real-time chat sessions.

Use technology to your advantage:

- Ensure all *collaboration devices are in working order.* Physically visit the room to test out the devices, especially the speaker phone and the projection system. You want to confirm any other room logistics, such as the presence of flip charts or markers, well *before* the meeting date. Have any missing or broken equipment replaced or repaired prior to the meeting.
- *Become an expert on the collaboration software and hardware* available to you. Understand how to display collaborative presentations and practice using whiteboard capabilities to display information in real time between a whiteboard and remote PCs. Take a look at 3M's dry-erase whiteboard[b], which has a computer projection screen for document or presentation.
- Learn how to *use the speaker phone.* There are many PC-based client-server software solutions that can effectively handle voice conferencing as well as video and slide sharing so you don't have to use a separate audio conferencing bridge service. AT&T has a range of conferencing services. Another resource are spiderphones, a Web-based audio-conferencing service, which allows up to 60 participants on a conference call with full access to their browsers.

- Check out *Web-based project collaboration software* for distributed teams. One popular tool is Basecamp[c]. Jitsi[d], a tool, to quickly show slides, capture ideas and comments in real time, and generally to ensure our meetings are effective. Microsoft Teams[e] is more interactive, allowing you to present to remote locations. Intel has piloted Live Meeting, and it is becoming the Intel standard. A free application-sharing and online meeting tool is WebEx[f]. These tools enable you to collaborate online in real time with just a PC and an Internet connection. These types of Web-based tools are excellent for retrospective meetings because many are very cost effective.
- *Web sites* are also an important part of an effective retrospective. A wiki makes it easy for anyone to post material or edit existing material. At Intel we use both wikis to encourage and simplify information exchange and collaboration among teams.

Conclusion

One effective method to help software development teams improve their software development practices is to conduct multiple retrospectives along the lifecycle to help uncover ways to *increase the effectiveness of the team by:*

- Sharing perspectives to understand what worked well in the project so we can reinforce it
- Identifying opportunities for improvement and lessons learned so they can improve the current and subsequent projects
- Making specific recommendations for changes
- Discussing what the team wants to do differently
- Helping the team see ways to work together more efficiently

By engaging with software development teams who are hungry for help to improve their processes, we continually focus on finding creative ways to work more efficiently and effectively. Globally dispersed teams are becoming more common. So, when the teams span several time zones and encompass many cultures, conducting a successful retrospective is very challenging.

At Intel, most software teams are located in different countries and in different states. By using all the technology and
resources available to us, we have been able to effectively
draw out from the teams what is working well, what needs
to be done differently next time, what we learned, and what
still puzzles us. Armed with this information we have been
able to develop action plans to improve and change the way
software is developed at Intel.

---

[a]Debra Lavell (USA), Intel Corporation, Organizational Learning & Retrospectives Program Manager.

[b]https://www.3m.com/3M/en_US/p/c/office-supplies/dry-
erase-bulletin-boards/i/consumer/

[c]https://basecamp.com/

[d]https://jitsi.org/

[e]https://www.microsoft.com/microsoft-teams/group-chat-
software

[f]https://www.webex.com

8.4 Metrics

Agile projects employ many kinds of metrics to measure project
status, progress, and the quality of the system under development. To generate meaningful data, teams must choose metrics
that are meaningful for the specific project. Although I have
worked on many projects, I almost never use the same set
of metrics for two projects. Typically, I start with metrics we
found useful on the previous project, then formulate a data
wish-list to guide information-gathering. Metrics not only help
teams identify internal progress and shortcomings, but also aid
visualizing external influences and their impact.

Progress Measurement

The Agile Manifesto stresses the importance of evaluating the
progress (velocity) of the diverse feature teams in light of
deliverables: "Working software is the primary measure of
progress."[10]

---

[10]Agile Manifesto online: http://agilemanifesto.org/principles.html.

Measuring meaningful progress can be a daunting task, but by looking at how well teams on a project perform together with respect to advancing to the project deadline as well as at how individual teams perform iteration by iteration, important predictors of a project's health can be identified. An individual team's overall performance normally is evaluated only in relation to that team's performance on past iterations as well as during the current iteration, with notice paid to any sizable discrepancies in performance from one iteration to another. Whatever the reasons for performance peaks and valleys, they must be measured and analyzed so that team progress can be stabilized. As has been noted, *comparing* the velocity of different feature teams is generally not feasible because some teams estimate features in an optimistic manner and others follow a more pessimistic path. Neither is it helpful to calculate features instead of points, because features typically are not of equal size, and measurements pertaining to them cannot be directly compared.[11] It is unproductive as well to compare progress made by dispersed versus collocated feature teams because a dispersed team normally needs more time than does a collocated team to come up to speed.

If you find that velocity stabilizes around, say, the fifth iteration for all feature teams except one, or that velocity improves for all teams except one, investigate whether the one team is hampered by some remediable challenge. On one of my projects, the exercise of measuring and comparing feature-teams' progress revealed that people on one team had serious skill problems. By supporting the team with two technical-skills mentors for a couple of iterations, we brought the team completely up to speed.

To measure progress, an agile project typically records the points a team earns at the end of an iteration for completed features, next records the point count as dots on a graph tracking that team's earned points for each iteration, and then takes the sum of points earned by all teams as the measure of progress for the whole project.[12] Thus, if one team earns 18 points on one iteration, 20 on the next, and 19 on the third, the points make a graph showing velocity for this team. Velocity for the whole project is derived by totaling the individual feature teams'

---

[11] Refer back to the previous chapter for a refresher on feature points.

[12] For more on computing the whole project's velocity and velocity disparities, see Chapter 7, "Ensuring Business Value."

points, which can then be used to predict the remaining course of the project. For example, if the whole project has a velocity of 100 complexity points per iteration and the complexity of all your remaining features sums up to 5,000 points, you will need 50 iterations for finalizing the product. Although your first prediction might not be very accurate, it will improve and get more realistic and precise with every iteration. Please note that this is not only getting more precise because the velocity stabilizes, but as well because you are getting a better understanding of what needs to be done.

Although I favor measuring project progress based on complexity points, it can also be helpful to measure based on number of features completed in an iteration, keeping in mind of course that feature size and complexity can vary greatly. I use this approach for projects on which agile methods are introduced partway through a project and features have already been estimated using a different approach than points. Instead of discarding past estimations, and re-estimating the features in points, I think it makes sense to use existing estimates to work within the project's measurement context.

To assess remaining work throughout a project's lifetime, agile practitioners can create a burn-down graph that depicts how many features have been delivered and how many are left to do for the next release as well as for the project to completion.[13] This graph is most often expressed in complexity points, but can be simplified to a count of features. For iterations, another graph shows tasks already done and those left to do.

---

[13]For more on measuring remaining work, see K. Schwaber and M. Beedle, *Agile Software Development with Scrum* (Englewood Cliffs, N.J.: Prentice-Hall, 2001).

Burndown Graph

Estimate-Quality Measurement

On my projects, for at least the first few iterations, and more if our teams have problems with realistic planning, we measure the *quality* of our estimates. In addition to gauging a team's velocity, we consider the difference between what velocity the team estimated and how close our perception was to reality. We measure this in complexity points *planned* versus complexity points *earned*. Whatever your unit of measurement, compare estimates with results. If your estimates are consistently proportionally off, turn that factor into a metric but not a multiplier. For example, if a team estimates one hundred hours but completes tasks for an iteration in two hundred hours, we don't compare estimated hours against hours worked and double every estimate. Instead, we use the experience as a guideline to adjust the estimation by the reduced (but actual) velocity to better reflect the reality of what can be accomplished in real time versus ideal time. It is fact that it is much easier for teams to estimate the way they are used to, and then adjust for interruptions that will prolong time to completion.

I find it helpful to visualize this mismatch to change team perception for future iterations and stimulate more realistic examination of team velocity, a tactic that proves especially useful on culturally diverse teams.[14] Illustrating the gap between work planned and work completed in an iteration helps a team to accept what it can really accomplish and deliver.

Increasing the Test Base

If a team is new to unit testing it is as well helpful to measure the growths in number of unit tests. Many teams experienced it as motivational to see how their test base grows. It shouldn't be necessary to measure successful tests against failed tests, because all tests should pass anyway. Yet, if your teams needs to get a hint that only successful tests are helpful, you might consider visualizing this as well.[15]

Again for teams new to unit testing a relative measurement showing the growths in number of (production – not testing) methods versus growths in number of unit tests, might be helpful to understand the relevance of testing.

A last measurement regarding testing that we use occasionally on our projects is test coverage.

8.5 Summary

Gathering feedback from iteration reviews, retrospectives, and especially customers is crucial for agile project success. Iteration reviews garner feedback regarding a system, including how well the efforts of feature teams integrate, how well teams work together, if tests succeed, if the system can be deployed outside the development environment, and more. Iteration reviews also provide feedback on estimate accuracy, from which to derive a realistic update for the overall project plan. Information shared

---

[14]For more on cultural differences with realistic planning, see Chapter 4, "Establishing Communication and Trust."

[15]Please see additional texts for more on testing, such as: *Perfect Software: and other Illusions about Testing* by Gerald M. Weinberg; *Five Core Metrics*, by Ware Myers and Laurence H. Putnam.

at iteration reviews shouldn't surprise anyone, but allow teams to analyze and benefit from feedback.

Retrospective feedback focuses on how team members and teams collaborate, identifying what helps individuals as well as the whole team move forward and what stumbling blocks they face. Teams develop action plans to improve performance. In this way, the retrospective is a means to actually shape the development process and better support both individuals' and teams' work efforts.

Although product owners provide valuable feedback from the customers' perspective, teams benefit from inviting stakeholders and end users, for example, to use the system under development. From this collaboration, project members learn how the customer will, in fact, use the system and the customer buys in to the development effort.

Measurements that show oscillating velocity signal a team that is experiencing trouble and can be used to reduce risk. Summing up the velocities of all feature teams helps forecast the time frame for the rest of the project and indicates whether the project can be finished on time or not. Visualizing features planned versus features completed helps teams learn to plan realistically.

9. Honing Practices

A man who plans to have a good impact,
has to seek for the best tools.

— Johann Wolfgang von Goethe

As in any agile environment, distributed agile development teams must find practices that support their value system. At the same time, in a distributed setting, all team members must be very disciplined following practices to keep all teams moving forward. For example, before members of a global team leave the office to go home, they must ensure that the system is integrated and running (a working build). Otherwise, other team members working in a different time zone won't be able to integrate their work into the shared codebase. Often projects fail because team members do not act in concert. One reason is that people are unaware of the big picture of a project. Each team member must understand his or her own stake and role in the project—and that of other team members and teams.

Many common development practices help establish and preserve the agile value system. Almost all agile practices were created for collocated teams. However, distributed teams can benefit from these practices once teams adapt them to their specific setting.

9.1 Development Practices

The Agile Manifesto stipulates that agile teams always ensure the highest-quality system: "continuous attention to technical excellence and good design enhances agility."[1] Below, I consider agile development practices that can be especially challenging in a global setting.

---

[1] Agile Manifesto online: http://agilemanifesto.org/principles.html.

Pair Programming

Pair programming, a practice frequently scrutinized and questioned within the development community, is one of the most effective agile practices. Pair programming generates not only continuous reviews but also disseminates knowledge about a project's domain, technology, and development culture. Collocated feature teams of a (large) distributed project that practice pair programming operate in much the same way as any small, local, agile team (in a non-distributed environment). Using pair programming on dispersed feature teams, however, could pose seemingly insurmountable problems. A colleague of mine reported about a successful approach with *virtual pair programming:* From two separate locations, he and his partnering programmer used virtual network computing (VNC), with each logging into the same remote machine that maintained the code base at a third location. This way, both programmers had the same bandwidth and access to the actual code.

One challenge programmers can encounter when pair programming virtually is maintaining full concentration. As Kircher and Levine observe, "The remote pair programmers are not physically adjacent, and therefore not as involved in the programming process. If there is sufficient communication delay, then pair programming could degrade to code review."[2]

When pair programming virtually, partners need to bridge the physical distance in order to see the same code, and communicate frequently and completely about what each is writing. Instant messaging, telephone or voice-over IP (such as Skype), and Web cams are tools that aid communication between remote pair programmers.[3] Another challenge of virtual pair programming is time difference. If coding partners work in dramatically different time zones, they can find it difficult to coordinate work schedules. Thus, most successful virtual pair programming occurs with pairs working in relatively close time zones.

---

[2]M. Kircher and D.L. Levine, "The XP of TAO: Extreme Programming of Large, Open-Source Frameworks," published in G. Succi and M. Marchesi, *Extreme Programming Examined* (Reading, Mass.: Addison-Wesley, 2001), p. 484. To view online, see http://www.kircher-schwanninger.de/michael/publications/xp2000.pdf.

[3]Skype is a free product that supports voice over the Internet, instant messaging, and video conferencing. See http://skype.org.

Different Timezones

An additional challenge of virtual pair programming arises when partners do not know each other very well, perhaps residing in different countries or working for different companies. Successful collaboration is difficult to achieve unless partners see each other frequently and share the same values and work ethic. The optimal setting for virtual pair programming is for colleagues to work from home offices a few days a week and meet in-person the rest of the week. By meeting face-to-face so frequently, partners constantly re-establish their relationship so it survives the adversities of virtual pair programming.

Other dispersed-team practitioners with virtual-pair-programming experience note that it is beneficial to regularly alternate between virtual pairing times and times at which programmers work alone, and recommend to form one consolidated work by merging each programmer's results after lone programming sessions jointly as a virtual pair. They further recommend conducting also the integration virtually together to reduce the possibility of error or failure.

Unit-Test

Agile teams verify every piece of production code (e.g. every method) with an automated unit test. Moreover, following what is commonly called a test-first approach, developers write and execute these unit tests not at the end of development but before the actual code is written. Hermann Mikula, Quality Manager of Computer Sciences Corporation in Klagenfurt, Austria, states the rationale for this approach simply: "At the end of development, you can't test quality into the system."[4] In fact, waiting to perform unit tests until the end of development can negatively impact the quality of the system, because people may just provide enough of a fix so that the code passes the test but does not contribute to overall system quality.

A benefit of having automated unit tests available for distributed projects is if the time difference between locations is rather large, it is often impossible to question a colleague if you don't understand how a piece of code works. Tests enable everyone to run quality checks of code and gain an understanding of how code works.

Refactoring

Continuous attention to refactoring, which is improving the internal structure of the code without changing the external behavior, is important for small, collocated teams, and even more so for large, distributed teams. If developers are not permanently watching out for refactoring areas that need to be cleaned up, the problems tend to get bigger and clean-up grows more costly. Adding new functionality in those areas is difficult and becomes even more problematic in a distributed and large setting. Refactoring later in development affects more areas and therefore more teams, requiring ever more coordination.

I recommend refactoring code iteratively, estimating refactoring along with other tasks at the beginning of an iteration. Do not explicitly name tasks "refactoring," but calculate refactoring as part of most tasks that complete a feature. If you must perform a grand refactoring because you ignored it earlier

---

[4]H. Mikula, personal communication.

while it was still small, try to be as transparent as possible about the need of it. Make the product owner aware of the refactoring, ensure he understands the necessity, risk, and cost of refactoring—and of not doing it. Generally, note that addressing grand refactorings are more costly than working on small ones.

Following are different strategies for grand refactorings – and please keep in mind that the best strategy is addressing small refactorings in order to avoid the grand ones:

- *Include the refactoring in your next iteration plan:* After making the product owner aware of the problem, the refactoring should be high-priority. However, the refactoring should be performed gradually. Try to avoid dedicating the entire next iteration solely to this refactoring; also deliver some business functionality.
- *Plan a refactoring iteration.* This is an iteration that's dedicated to refactoring only. There are different possibilities to perform such a refactoring iteration:
    - *Schedule it during a special time:* Schedule a refactoring iteration at a slack time when it will least impact progress on new business functionality (for instance, during vacation time or holidays).
    - *Plan a short iteration:* If your iterations normally last two weeks, plan a one-week refactoring iteration. We use here often iterations that are naturally shortened because of holidays. This will allow your team and customers not to delay new business functionality a whole iteration.
- *Assemble a refactoring team:* Set up a refactoring team in parallel with other teams: This team can work in parallel with other feature teams and conduct refactoring while others ensure progress on business functionality. This strategy can be combined with the first approach, where refactoring is just one part of the iteration plan. A colleague of mine works on a project with several feature teams developing new functionality and one refactoring team that cleans up afterward.
- *Convene a refactoring team during off hours:* The refactoring team operates only for a specific amount of time, outside regular working hours, working at such times would allow team members to make necessary changes all at once, without interrupting the regular development.[5]

---

[5]For more on refactoring, see Eckstein, op. cit., p. 149.

These strategies' greatest advantage is that the refactoring gets completed, and as a consequence the system is easier to maintain. Disadvantages include slowing progress and restricting knowledge of good programming style. Consider rotating refactoring team members to disseminate this knowledge. The most sustainable approach is for every team member to continuously monitor the need for refactoring and work on it as soon as it is recognized.

Refactoring on Large Projects: How Cleaners Became the Experts in Programming by Nicolai M. Josuttis[a]

Some time ago, I joined a large team of software developers responsible for maintaining customer data for an international mobile phone company. The primary goal was to manage customers in a way that they could have phone calls and get appropriately billed. Although the software was relatively young, we had to refactor it to avoid a situation where it became no longer maintainable, a casualty of the rapidly growing market for mobile phones (there were other things to do than to invest in the code quality).

Improving code quality is done via refactoring, which means modifying code while keeping its purpose and business functionality. However, of course, we could not stop the usual code evolution while refactoring it; business had to go on. Therefore, we had to fulfill parallel requirements, on one hand adding new features and modifying business logic and on the other hand cleaning up existing features while keeping existing business logic.

The first thing we learned was that it was not enough to refactor the code so as to provide better frameworks and libraries with new and improved interfaces and programming patterns. Again and again, we found that developers didn't use the new, improved interfaces to implement their code, but continued to use the old, deprecated interfaces. The reason for the behavior was simple. Nowadays, there is in principle only one common form of programming: copy-and-paste. When developers have to program a specific piece of code to fulfill a new business requirement, they start by searching for an existing solution that does almost the same or at least something similar. Then, they copy this code and modify it for their specific purpose. So, they copy the old, deprecated way to solve things.

So, the first lesson was that, as a general rule, refactorings did not end with providing better interfaces. For a refactoring of an interface, it became a general rule that those who provide a new interface also have to ensure that the old, deprecated interface is not used any longer. This, by the way, has two important advantages: You see whether your new interface really works in all existing contexts, and you can remove the old interface and not have to maintain deprecated code.

But this policy also has some drawbacks. First, you violate the "never change a running system" principle. This, for example, means that you have to run all the tests that ensure that the new behavior matches the old behavior. Second, you need additional resources because testing in large systems always includes significant manual effort.

Next, the question came up: How do you ensure that existing applications of the old interfaces get modified? If such a change is performed by members of the team providing the new interface, they will need specific business knowledge of the existing application of the old interface. In addition, the team providing the new interface might not be permitted to modify other programmers' code. This leads to the question, whether there is collective code ownership or whether, for each piece of code, specific people are responsible for it? In any case, collaboration is required (either to let different people modify existing (foreign) code and ensure the corresponding knowledge is communicated or to manage code modifications between different people (who are the owners of these pieces of code)).

Finally, the following question came up: How do you deal with the parallel modifications for new features and those due to refactoring? It turned out that handling the refactoring task just like any other task for adding a new feature did cause some problems. An obvious problem was that modifications for new features always had a higher priority. Or, to formulate it differently, if people have to choose between an investment in the maintainability of the code in the future and a change that allows them to sell or offer a new requested feature, new features always win. Having the same people doing both kinds of tasks brought this dilemma up again and again in the day-to-day programmer's life.

As a consequence, we made an important decision. We separated those who code new features from those who clean up the code. This resolved the unclear priorities for the individual programmer. Programmers responsible for adding new features could concentrate on this task by using their usual copy-and-paste approach. Programmers responsible for refactorings to improve the code quality concentrated on modifying things while keeping the existing behavior.

Note that the effort for a refactoring is usually harder to predict (you start with a tiny clean-up and get a chain reaction of associated refactorings). Now, as the refactoring team was independent from the team adding new features, incorrect predictions for refactoring did not delay new features scheduled next.

In essence, we established an interesting process: There were those people adding new features and making the code more and more messy. And there were those people trying to do their best to clean up this mess. In principle, this separation of concerns worked well, but it takes a special kind of person to do the refactoring job. It's like a cleaner who remains happy cleaning the same things again and again, all the while wondering how others can make so much mess. Such a person has to be a pedant or stickler instead of a curriculum vitae-driven architect who wants to try every new hype.

Of course, it helps to understand that everybody creates mess. So, exchanging team members between feature teams and the refactoring team is usually a good idea as it facilitates communication about things different people deal with. However, note that programmers who have problems doing something else than copy-and-paste (which might not be their fault as they, for example, might do not have had enough time to understand the complexity of the code) should not perform the complex code clean-ups. In programming, cleaning is something for the experts.

[a]Nicolai M. Josuttis (Germany), http://josuttis.com

Collective Ownership

Collective ownership means that every member of the team cares in the same way and has responsibility for every artifact, including code, and can make changes to any artifact as needed. *Exclusive ownership* means that a team member can only make changes to his or her own artifacts, a practice guaranteed to introduce severe bottlenecks, if, for instance, a change needs to be made to a specific artifact or part of the code and the owner is not around. In such cases, everybody else has to either wait or work around the problem. Exclusive ownership can also cause head monopolies, where knowledge about any given artifact is only in the mind of the owner. If a global project is small with, say, fewer than three sub-teams, I recommend following the collective-ownership approach.

For large, distributed teams just as on large, collocated teams, a variety of exclusive ownership called *team ownership* works best, giving every team exclusive ownership of every artifact developed by its members while providing team members with collective ownership of all artifacts developed by their team-mates.[6] I find that this strategy protects code integrity and maintains responsibility while allowing team members adequate access to make changes and fix errors.

Of course, if members of a single feature team work for different companies, they may be hindered by their employers' service-level agreement (SLA). In such a case, the best approach is to ask employers to change their SLAs to accommodate shared, team ownership. If modifying an SLA is not feasible, each member of the feature team can assume exclusive responsibility for a specific artifact or part of the code and ask peers to create a branch to permit implementing changes to the part. [7] The exclusive owner will then verify and release this branch with the support of the version control system. As this work-around is not very straightforward, I recommend implementing team ownership directly.

Common Coding Guideline

I recommend every project—no matter whether local or global— has a common coding guideline in place, without which, maintaining the system becomes a nightmare. People more willingly adhere to the guideline if it is kept short and crisp, and if they

---

[6] For more on artifacts ownership, see Eckstein, op. cit., p. 141.

[7] A branch is a planned split in the path of a versioned element (that is, of a method or class as defined in object-oriented development. Both paths of the element can be further version controlled.

can use tools that automatically verify adherence. When people resist working according to the coding guideline, it is generally because the guideline is overwhelming in size and doesn't support their objectives. In such a case, ask the developers to improve it.[8]

Feature Communication via Tests

On a distributed project following a traditional, linear, waterfall approach, a team at one location typically prepares a detailed software or system specification to send to a team at a second site who studies the specification and tries to implement it. At a predetermined milestone, the second site delivers work developed according to its interpretation of the requirements specification. Because there is little communication between sites, development is based on (often incorrect) assumptions, and the product developed does not satisfy the customer.

An agile approach, however, defines requested features in the form of acceptance tests. The philosophy behind this idea is that teams have to develop acceptance tests anyway at some point, so detailing features for a specification and then also for tests is redundant. Furthermore, acceptance tests are typically more accurate, less ambiguous, and incorporate fewer risks of misunderstanding than written specifications. And finally, the acceptance tests have the big advantage (after the implementation of the corresponding code) of being executable. This enables remote teams to find out for themselves if they understand the requirements by just executing this kind of "specification". Keith Braithwaite and Tim Joyce recommend this strategy: "Use failing functional tests to express the required functionality. The requirement is expressed unambiguously." [9]

At the foundation of this communication approach is an acceptance-testing framework that allows team members to define executable tests and is still readable (FIT and FitNesse are viable examples[10]). Other strategies that support this approach

---

[8]For further discussion, see Eckstein, op. cit., p. 151.

[9]Keith Braithwaite and Tim Joyce. XP Expanded: Distributed Extreme Programming. In: Proceedings of XP 2005. Springer Verlag 2005. Quoted from p. 187

[10]FIT and FitNesse are both open-source tools. See http://fit.c2.com and http://fitnesse.org. For an explanation of how to use FIT, see R. Mugridge and W. Cunningham, *Fit for Developing Software: Framework for Integrated Tests* (Upper Saddle River, N.J.: Pearson Education, 2005).

are the domain experts and testers to work closely together at the site where acceptance tests are developed. Ideally, domain experts have experience writing acceptance tests, but this is rarely the case. On two of my projects, domain experts developed all acceptance tests; however, we generally needed testers to then edit and eliminate errors from those tests.

This practice is used mainly by global projects with one or several offshore-outsourced teams, which makes it often difficult to convince those teams to fully adopt an agile approach. Generally, the goal is always to integrate each and every team fully in the agile process. In such a setting, every feature team will have a product owner who steers the iterations through features, clarifies upcoming questions, and accepts or rejects the accomplishments at the end of the iteration. The communication of feature requirements through tests is then an additional approach to the verbal communication about the requirements between the product owner and the team.

Distributed Agile and Acceptance Testing by Naresh Jain[a]

Back in 2004, I was working from Bangalore for a New York based client. Our client was building a pay-per-view product for cable companies in the U.S. and Europe. The product consisted of various components, which were built using different technologies. The piece of the product that my team was working on was the heart of the whole system. It was an Enterprise Application Integration (EAI) project for a back-office data validation and billing system. It also had components of the J2EE stack for presentation. A four member team from Bangalore worked on this project for 20 months with a client principal in New York. From the client side, we had a project manager, a subject-matter expert, a DBA, and two testers. The team was new to Extreme Programming and was exploring some of its practices.

Decreased communication bandwidth, lack of visibility into the project status, lack of trust, loss of business context, and delayed feedback are some of the most common challenges distributed development teams face. The consequences of these challenges can be quite severe. These problems exist in a collocated team as well, but in a distributed environment, the impact gets amplified. In the following section, based on my experience on various distributed project over the last six years, I'll highlight some key learning of how we combated these challenges.

When we started on this project, all of us in Bangalore were new to the concept of pay-per-view. None of us had ever used a pay-per-view system. In short, we all lacked the domain knowledge. So when the subject-matter expert explained a user story, we're not able to relate to most of the things they described. Because we were too embarrassed to say "we don't understand," we would say "OK, we understand," and we would end up building something very different from what our client wanted us to build. Initially, we also had difficultly understanding the accent of the client-side members, which added to our misunderstandings. While we were struggling with all these issues, we discovered the magic of acceptance tests and test-driven development.

Traditionally, we gather requirements and then, once the product was built, we had a user-acceptance-test phase where customers would try to use the real system and check if it meets their needs and if they would accept the product. Since the feedback cycle is very long, some teams try to have a customer review after each phase of the software development process. Unfortunately, until customers look at the product, they cannot make much sense of what is happening. In my experience, this approach leads to hell breaking loose at the end of the project.

Acceptance testing was a solution to avoid this problem. Acceptance testing is an Extreme Programming (XP) practice, where the customer (defined as the person who initiates a user story) specifies acceptance criteria along with the user story (call it "requirements" if you like the word better). The acceptance criteria describe conditions under which the customer would accept the story and declare it as functionally complete. Once the team has acceptance criteria, it can collaborate with the customer to get examples for each of the criteria and to automate these checks. These automated units are referred to as acceptance tests. Tools like FIT and FitNesse help you achieve this.

Initially, we took a few stories and wrote acceptance tests ourselves using FIT. Once we had it working, we demonstrated it to our customers. Surprisingly, they liked the approach and got on board with it. The beauty of the automated acceptance tests and the collaborative authoring process is that they eradicate ambiguity in the requirement and help the development team be on the same page as the customer. This can be really helpful for distributed teams because now they are forced to collaborate more with the customer and also they provide a clear ending point for feature development. When all the acceptance tests work, the story is functionally complete. So not just does this help with the poor communication bandwidth, but it also helps to increase project status visibility. The customer could easily run these acceptance tests or look at our continuous integration reports to see the status of current work in progress. Over a period of time, these acceptance tests started contributing as regression tests.

While all this sounds great, we hit a roadblock, and we had to abandon this practice on our team. We started off using FIT with a library for testing HTML pages. Basically, our FIT tests would manipulate Web pages using this homegrown library. Writing acceptance tests at the Web layer seemed like the right thing to do when we started, but it turned out that our acceptance tests were very fragile. It got us started very quickly, but we were spending too much time maintaining acceptance tests, to the point, that it seemed an overkill. We still continued the collaboration aspect of acceptance tests, but stopped writing/maintaining any acceptance tests.

When I moved to a new distributed project, based on this learning, we started writing acceptance tests one layer below the graphical user interface. Surprisingly, this time it worked beautifully. It worked so well that, since then, I have been using this practice on all my projects, even collocated ones.

Following is the description of how this practice works in a distributed set-up.

Before the iteration begins, the customer (or product owner), along with the help of business analysts (or subject-matter experts), would come up with user stories and acceptance criteria for each of the stories. During the planning meeting, the product owner or analyst would explain the story and the acceptance criteria to the development team. Acceptance criteria enormously helped us clarify things. Sometimes, if the story was not clear, we would have a discussion and add new acceptance criteria or update existing acceptance criteria to remove any ambiguity. Once the expected functionality was clear, the developers would use the acceptance criteria to size the stories appropriately, which in-turn helped to estimate the story. With the help of the estimates and priorities, the whole team would commit to user stories.

During iterations, the developers would pick stories and block time with the customer or the subject-matter expert to write examples for acceptance criteria. These were usually hour-long meetings over the Internet, called "Deep Dive" sessions. Since FitNesse provides a wiki, and most of our customers were familiar with wikis, we would collaborate on the wiki to write examples for acceptance criteria. With the help of the wiki and an instant messenger (sometimes VoIP), we were able to create the examples for the given story. Usually, we would also have testers involved at this step; based on this understanding, the testers could come up with their test scripts (mostly automated) for testing.

From here, the developers would go off and develop the story, while the testers would work on other test cases for the same story. Once the developers were done, the testers would run all their tests and sign off on the story. At the end of the iteration, the customer would participate in the showcase and sign-off on all the stories that were completed.

There were times when the story was ready, but the testers found some issues or the customer asked the development team to change some stuff. Acceptance tests do not guarantee 100-percent, bullet-proof functionality. The goal is to help drive development and catch the obvious mistakes that otherwise slip by till the end. I remember a case where we were building some functionality to sort all the records that were displayed, based on columns. We had working acceptance tests, and the customer looked at the demo and was happy. Once we delivered it, it came back with a bug. In the production environment, there were a lot of records in the database and the results were paginated. The problem was, we were only sorting current-page rows, but the customer wanted to sort rows in all the pages. Things like this can be missed, but our existing tests gave us the safety net and confidence to jump in and make the change.

Acceptance testing has helped us reduce communication gaps and improve the visibility of the project. Try it a couple of times to believe in it.

---

[a]Naresh   Jain   (India),   Post   Modern   Agilist,

Out-of-the-Box Practices

I absolutely recommend using an established agile process as a guidance. To my mind, XP is the most powerful agile process in respect of defined development practices and it is a good idea to aim for using those practices as well on global projects.

Teams might struggle to implement recommended development practices successfully, but this is not a problem as long as they remember the values and principles of agility stated in the Agile Manifesto. When considering change development practices, teams should follow three steps:

- *Study the objectives of the practice:* A team should examine the objectives of a practice. If, for instance, pair programming is the practice a team is struggling with, then, the team might identify the objectives of pair programming as knowledge transfer, higher discipline, and better quality via continuous reviews.
- *Decide if objectives match your own:* Next, a team has to decide if the objectives of a practice match their own. Continuing the example above, team members might decide that they would like to achieve the goals of knowledge transfer, higher discipline, and better quality in spite of problems they encounter implementing pair programming.
- *Define practices that promote own goals:* Assuming the team decides that the objectives of the practice match their own, it then must ensure using practices supporting these goals. This could mean that the team defines two or more practices to ensure an out-of-the-box practice objective—for example, for reaching the goals of pair programming the team might decide on peer reviews, on a rule that everything needs to be seen by two sets of eyes, on code inspections, on regular code readings, and many other things. The team might agree on all of these strategies together to aim for the same objectives the single practice pair programming aims for.

Always try an out-of-the-box practice before deciding that a specific practice will not work. Start for example implementing the XP development practices and when struggling gradually adapt them for your environment.

9.2 Process Practices

Most of the time, collocated teams synchronize naturally (for example, through conversations at the water cooler, overhearing conversations during work and exchanging information over coffee). Such informal, highly important conversations can't happen on distributed projects. Enabling synchronization across a whole project is tough if the project is heavily distributed. Therefore, information exchanges have to be institutionalized. You have to enable synchronization, otherwise every site will try to reach for its own goals which is hardly aligned with the overall project's goals. Below I explain synchronization strategies that support large distributed projects.

Daily Synchronization (Daily Scrum)

In general, every software development team, small or large, dispersed or collocated, must synchronize on a daily basis to succeed. Daily synchronization is a part of all agile processes. (In Extreme Programming, this is called the Daily Stand-Up meeting; in Scrum, the Daily Scrum; in feature-driven development,[11] the Morning Roll Call; and in Dynamic Systems Development,[12] the Daily Wash-Up.) These terms stress *daily* performance.

Daily synchronization usually takes only ten to fifteen minutes. In this short meeting, team members report individually on the following:

- what they have worked on since the last synchronization (yesterday)
- what they will work on until the next synchronization (tomorrow)
- what (expected) impediments hinder their work

---

[11] Feature-driven development: http://www.featuredrivendevelopment.com.
[12] For the Dynamic Systems Development Method, see http://dsdm.org.

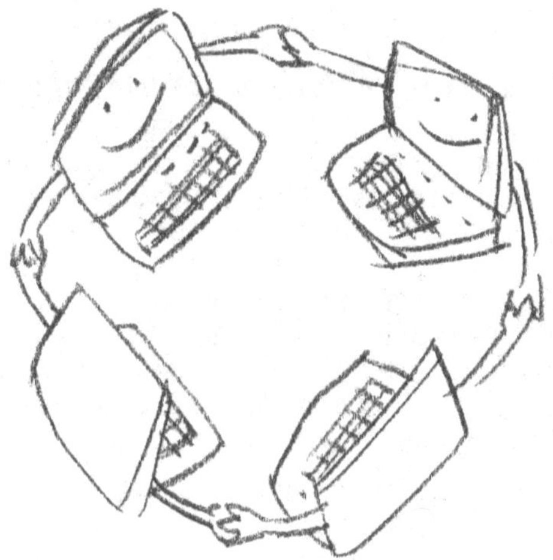

Daily Synchronization

The daily synchronization provides feedback on the current status of the project. It supports dealing with roles, or finding out about possible problems early on. Yet, this meeting is not about solving problems. Whenever a team member reports impediments, decide when and who will help resolve the issue and ensure to follow-up on the issue. The solution might be an escalation towards management, a quick design session with a team mate, or a phone call with the customer, just anything that helps this team member to get her job done. However, if you try to solve problems at the daily synchronization, it is very difficult to keep meetings short and to the point. Long daily synchronizations result in boring the participants and in (justifiably) questioning the usefulness of these meetings. Daily synchronization is a status exchange among peers, so all team members gain the same understanding about development progress.

To help keep meetings short, XP favors conducting the daily synchronization as a stand-up meeting. This is to literally keep team members on their toes, rather than lulled in their seats at a conference table. Dedicate one person to enforce efficiency rules for the daily synchronization. This could be just some team member, yet very often this responsibility is taken by the team's coach.

Project-Wide Synchronization (Scrum of Scrums)

The daily synchronization serves team members' need to develop a common understanding about each person's tasks on a feature team. However, if the project consists of more than one feature team, you also need to ensure transmission of information across different feature teams. This is performed by a project-wide synchronization meeting known by Scrum as a (daily) Scrum of Scrums. It has, generally, the same structure as the daily synchronization. Each feature team selects one representative to attend the Scrum of Scrums.

Similar to the daily synchronization, representatives report individually on the following:

- what their feature team has worked on since the last synchronization yesterday)
- what the feature team will work on until the next synchronization (tomorrow)
- what (expected) impediments hinder the feature team's work

Also this project-wide synchronization should be kept within ten to fifteen minutes. Colleagues and I have been able to keep this meeting down to fifteen minutes even with about twenty representatives participating. The key is not to transition from reporting to discussion. Representatives simply exchange status, and then report back to their teams so every team is aware of the whole project status.

Depending on the complexity of project team structure, establish different levels of synchronization. For instance, a feature team's daily synchronization is the first level of information transmission. The second level might be the Scrum of Scrums (the information exchange between all feature teams). Larger projects may not be able to accommodate all feature teams in one meeting. These projects can introduce another level of synchronization. For example, just feature teams focusing on a specific domain could synchronize in a Scrum of Scrums, and then representatives of all domains on a project could exchange information in a Scrum of Scrum of Scrums.

The more complex the project structure, the more likely that higher levels of synchronization (the Scrum of Scrum of Scrums, say) will overlook important information. To prevent obscurity or loss of information, invite representatives from another synchronization level (or a different feature team or domain), to join as listeners in regular daily synchronizations. Instead of organizing a Scrum of Scrums with the feature teams from a domain A, and then a Scrum of Scrum of Scrums across all domains, I invite interested people from other domains to come and listen in during the Scrum of Scrums of domain A.

On some of my projects, we find it helpful to have a Site Scrum of Scrums where feature team representatives located at the same site synchronize. This Site Scrum of Scrums is not held daily—meeting once or twice a week allows time to clarify specific site-related issues (most often infrastructure-related or about local politics).

Dispersed Synchronization

Synchronization is acutely important for dispersed projects. To ensure that everyone is on the same page, use synchronization meetings to make up for the lack of water-cooler conversation and other informal information transmission that serves as the glue of collocated projects. Keep everyone informed by using low-tech solutions, such as setting up a daily telephone conference call. On my projects, we plan for dispersed synchronizations by considering the following:

- *Connect via telephone:* Connect to other sites via telephone (conference call).
- *Use a speaker and microphone:* Provide each conference-call room with a quality speaker and microphone. Avoid using the telephone instead of a microphone. I have learned that as soon as people speak into a phone, they forget the larger audience and speak as if in a one-on-one conversation. This might prolong the meeting as well as cause speakers to neglect careful, detailed explanations, or to speak too quickly or advanced for non-native listeners to understand.

- *Prepare brief reports:* If twenty or more people take part in a dispersed daily synchronization, support the meeting by asking attendees to prepare a brief report for dissemination over the project wiki. This preparation should take only one to two minutes—it's not meant to be a full-fledged report. Since synchronization takes place on a daily basis, this is just a quick update.
- *Take notes:* Select one participant to take notes on impediments requiring follow-up. Post notes in a visible, accessible place for everybody to read (for example, on the project's wiki).
- *Share the iteration plan:* Use a collaboration platform so everyone can see the iteration plan during a dispersed synchronization meeting.
- *Be creative:* On one of my projects, all team members understood but could barely speak the language of the main site, Austria. For some of the team members, this language was even their second or third language. We decided to level the playing field: Everybody had to speak in a non-native language with the choices of English and German. The Austrians spoke English, and the Hungarians spoke either German or English (whatever they preferred). This helped everyone clarify and understand what we talked about, because everyone spoke more slowly and used simpler vocabulary than was customary. Seek creative methods to ensure that synchronization meetings effectively transfer information and team members are mutually respectful.
- *Allow extra time:* To strengthen bonds within a dispersed team, allow time during the daily synchronization for informal conversations.[13] This strategy allows participants to talk about what they care about—a problem on the project, their families and friends, or other interests.

---

[13]Thanks to Jamie Allsop for pointing this out.

Time for informal conversations

While it may seem to offer people a more direct channel of communication and opportunity for getting to know each other, videoconferencing turns out to be more hindrance than help—or so my experience has demonstrated. Because of the different time zones, some people might just have woken up, and others are ready to go to bed. Some projects do benefit from a video connection during synchronization meetings, especially in a project's early stages before people recognize each other's voices.

If the phone works well for connecting distant people, what is the best way for connecting a group of collocated people to distant individuals. There are actually two approaches for involving collocated people in a conference call with remote members, and both have to be considered carefully:

- *Collocated people meet in person.* One possibility is for collocated team members to meet in person in the same room every day and connect to the rest of the team via phone. For example, some members of a dispersed team might meet in a room in Germany, some in Russia, and some in Ireland. A conference call between Germany, Russia, and Ireland will connect the different rooms. This setting enforces social presence at least among the collocated people. If this synchronization refers to a Scrum of Scrums, then these participants belong to different feature teams and thus this in-person meeting improves trust and mutual respect between these teams. However, using this strategy you have to ensure that the participants who meet in person are not conducting any side conversations or using body language, because all of these would exclude all distant parties.

- *Everybody uses the same bandwidth.* The second possibility is for every team member to participate in the dispersed synchronization in the same manner. Thus, all participants connect with the highest conjointly available bandwidth. This is especially important when trust is essential, because otherwise always the ones with the worst bandwidth are left behind. For example, if at one site resides only one member of a dispersed feature team, who can only connect via the phone, then although there might be other team members located at different sites who could meet in person or participate via video conferencing, everyone will connect via the phone (using their headsets). This might sound stupid at first, but if decided otherwise always the ones with the weakest connection will have the biggest issues participating. Thus for respecting everyone on the team and not preferring one over the other the same technology should be used across all sites.[14]

The daily synchronization, as the term implies, should take place every day, at the same time, and at the same location (or should use the same conference call phone number). Find a time amenable to everyone, even if the team is dispersed. Scott Ambler suggests "to negotiate overlapping blocking times; for example, your London team is available in their late afternoon and your New York team in their early morning to schedule teleconference and videoconference meetings as needed." [15] Most agile methods recommend that the synchronization meeting takes place at the same time every day, yet if a team is

---

[14]Thanks to Ainsley Nies for sharing this insight at Agile Open North West, Portland, Oregon, USA in 2007

[15]Scott Ambler. Bridging the Distance. Dr.Dobb's Portal. August 2002. (http://www.ddj.com/dept/architect/184414899)

dispersed, however, it sometimes helps if you *don't* stick to the "same time every day" rule. Instead, decide on different times for each weekday. This way, the timing is comfortable for every attendee at least some of the time, not just for people located at the main site.

Ensure to schedule the dispersed daily synchronization using a round-robin strategy. For time differences of twelve hours, the only possible meeting times are very early in the morning or very late in the evening. Still, I recommend to swap the meeting times so it is not very early for the same people all the time – unless all participants have clear preferences that are in sync (e.g. on the one site of the globe people prefer early morning meetings and on the other site late evening meetings). For time differences of more than twelve hours, establish a "satellite" to compensate for the difference. For example, to bridge the time difference between California and China, have a satellite team in Europe ensure communication back and forth, by attending two daily synchronizations. Dispersed participants can also answer the three synchronization questions on the project wiki. On one of my projects this was the only possibility for one of the dispersed feature teams. On another project, we used this strategy to reduce the length of dispersed synchronization meetings. Then we could focus mainly on uncovering impediments while keeping meetings short. Using a satellite team will not solve your problem completely, because having an indirection often makes communication more complex. I recommend to additionally ensure your bond via longer face-to-face meetings and to use electronic media in the time between those face-to-face meetings. For the frequency of the face-to-face meetings you have to take the threshold for trusted connections into account.[16] Many global projects are only able to keep a good communication flow between different sites with huge time differences, because enough project members have different bio rhythms. Thus, some of them prefer to work late at night where others prefer extremely early mornings. These people help to expand the time overlap between different sites.

Lise Hvatum suggests conducting Smart Meetings as another way to build informal communication channels and promote social bonds: "By allocating common time and making team members available to each other at agreed times during the

---

[16] More on the threshold for trusted connections in Chapter 4 *Communication and Trust*.

week, you can mimic spontaneous contact (albeit with a delay)."[17] Although pre-scheduled, Smart Meetings should only be conducted if participants have something to talk about, and can be scheduled in conjunction with dispersed synchronization meetings.

9.3 Development Culture

Distance makes everything that distributed teams want to have in common more difficult to ensure. Distance also complicates efforts to establish a joint development culture, meaning a development culture accepted across all teams and sites. Only such a joint culture allows delivering one coherent, maintainable product, not several products. By establishing and following a joint development culture, projects will not only have fewer problems developing one coherent product, but also those people who will be responsible for maintaining the product will as well have less difficulty.

It is much easier to jointly learn and make use of synergies if there is agreement on rules for development such that the culture is the same at all locations and for all teams. Culture, however, cannot be dictated. In order to create this joint culture, team members themselves must determine the rules under which all will willingly function. But this is not all to it; from time to time, all members of the dispersed and distributed teams must look carefully at the agreement to revisit what really works and what doesn't as well as what's really accepted and what isn't.

Project-Wide Practices

On global projects, I find that practices such as the following help us to evolve and maintain a project-wide common development culture:

- *Make how-to's available on the project wiki:* This posting of information helps team members who are new either to the project or to a specific technical or domain area find their way more rapidly, but it also helps *all* team

---

[17]L.B. Hvatum, op. cit., p. 8.

members remember what's integral to the development culture. Everyone on the team has to take responsibility to update tutorials, comments, and guides to project tasks if necessary. The coach might have to remind project members on this responsibility whenever somebody starts complaining about outdated how-to's.

- *Evolve patterns from retrospectives and reviews:* During retrospectives, we spend much effort on discovering what helps and what hinders team members when working together.[18] Reviews help detecting common mistakes and great solutions. From these, we develop a do's and don'ts guide to post on the project wiki where it is easy to change or add to throughout the project.

- *Mentors enable adherence to the common culture:* While a team coach generally helps team members stick to the rules of their agreed-upon culture (or change the agreements if they are no longer valid), appointing experienced and knowledgeable team member to serve as mentor can increase the project's probability of success. Mentors benefit protégés not only by their experience and advice but also their encouragement to adopt and adapt project culture, especially if changes in attitude are required, as for example test-driven development requests. Of course in some cases, regular training classes could also help acquiring such knowledge. Yet, more often you will find that a training class is too much of an artificial environment and that newbies on a specific task or attitude need direct support in their daily work.

Communication facilitators will help creating a common culture and detecting difficulties with agreements. They have to ensure that the knowledge about some learnings in one team will be spread and made available to other teams on the global project.[19]

Changing Practices

The preceding practices help distributed projects establish a common culture, but in order to keep it viable, teams need to

---

[18]Retrospectives are discussed in greater detail in Chapter 8, "Eliciting Feedback and Conducting Retrospectives."

[19]Communication facilitators are discussed in greater detail in Chapter 5, "Keeping Sites in Touch."

inspect and improve rules and behaviors based on information gathered at regularly scheduled meetings and, from time to time, at project retrospectives. On most distributed projects, (changing) team representatives meet regularly (in person or virtually) to assess whether all teams are following the rules and guidelines of their agreed-upon joint development culture. If the common culture is being watered down or even partially ignored, teams need to seek out the underlying cause. Areas to investigate include whether team members have forgotten specifics or lack adequate skills to fulfill their responsibilities, do not accept the agreements, or whether guidelines have become unwieldy, outdated, or completely obsolete as development progresses. If agreements are not accepted by team members they are by default invalid. In such a situation representatives have to analyze the importance of these agreements and decide on necessary changes so that they will be accepted and followed.

Sometimes, agreed-upon practices are followed by one feature team but not by any other. The representative from the feature team successfully using a specific practice needs to report how they mentored and established use of the practice and, even more important, what the team's experience has been.

Different Practices

Although we aim for exactly the same development culture across all sites and teams, it is not always realistic to achieve. It is more practical to agree on a set of principles and allow implementation details to differ, and teams to customize development practices.

On one of my projects some feature teams applied test-driven development and others didn't. We never experienced this as a problem as long as all teams agreed to only integrate their code with existing tests. Thus the tests were always developed promptly – some teams developed them before the code and some right afterwards. Another example refers to a different project, where one feature team used pair programming heavily whereas another feature team preferred to ensure the quality of the code and the knowledge transfer through code inspections. But only these overall principles give us the freedom for different development cultures in the diverse feature teams without hurting ourselves.

However, it should be obvious that one feature team cannot

go rogue and, for example, use an integration platform or strategy that is different from one being used by peer teams because of the negative impact this change would have on peer teams. A different development culture can be followed by diverse feature teams as long as it doesn't affect the other teams. Communication among teams about how changes could affect each other's work must be continuously monitored. I do recommend that teams report successful practices that might help other teams struggling with similar issues. Inherent in the definition of "successful" is that a practice is effective and does not harm another team's efforts. A frequent exchange across feature teams on the usage of practices will contribute to continuous learning and enable the whole team to get more effective.

Process Standards based on CMMI or ISO

Many books about global development discuss harmonizing the development process between sites only within the context of ISO or Carnegie-Mellon Software Engineering Institute's CMMI[20] standards.[21] This restricted view assumes that offshore teams are certified CMMI level 4 or higher and that before going offshore the main site should as well be certified at least CMMI level 3 or higher. The expectation is that certification ensures harmonization of team methodologies. For the following reasons, I view such assumptions as naïve: CMMI certifications do not confirm flexibility and willingness to collaborate, nor do they guarantee development quality—rather, they merely confirm that the certified party follows CMMI-described processes. If an SEI-certified process is an agile one, flexibility will probably be built into the process, but this is just another assumption.

One conflict between agile and CMMI is that CMMI often is counterproductive to innovation. Prabhudev Konana, a professor at the University of Texas at Austin, notes, "rigid processes such as CMM certification that have helped [firms] to become known for quality might not necessarily encourage innovation. In fact, rigidity can stifle unconventional practices even when

---

[20]CMMI – Capability Maturity Model Integration.

[21]For detailed information about global (but not necessarily agile) software development, see C. Ebert, *Outsourcing kompakt* (Heidelberg: Elsevier, 2006) and E. Carmel's *Global Software Teams: Collaborating Across Borders and Time Zones* (Englewood Cliffs, N.J.: Prentice-Hall, 1999).

they might have a positive influence on innovation."[22]

This is not to discredit certification, but to encourage teams to recognize the limitations and false confidence of certification. Following are several frictions that differentiate agile from CMMI approaches:

- CMMI is process-driven whereas agility is people-driven (recall the first value comparison in the Agile Manifesto: "Individuals and interactions over processes and tools[23]).
- CMMI requires strict adherence to process whereas agility requires teams to regularly question the process in place.[24]

- CMMI requests intense activity tracking whereas agility focuses on meeting goals and therefore tracks progress and deliveries instead of activities.[25]
- CMMI encourages documentation quantity whereas agility requests light documentation.[26]

The combination of certain aspects of CMMI and agility can be beneficial, however. Jakobsen reports, "CMMI can help agile companies to institutionalize agile methods more consistently and understand what processes to address. ... Scrum and other agile methodologies can guide such companies towards more efficient implementation of CMMI process requirements."[27]

Jakobsen further elaborates that the foundation for combining CMMI and agile is based on the fact that both help to establish a culture and value system of continuous improvement. CMMI keeps the focus on *what* kind of process should be applied, while an agile approach concentrates on *how* processes should be performed. CMMI and agile each on its own will provide great

---

[22] P. Konana, "Can Indian Software Firms Compete with the Global Giants?" *IEEE Computer,* (July 2006), p. 45.

[23] See the Agile Manifesto online: http://agilemanifesto.org.

[24] abid. Principle of the Manifesto: "*At regular intervals, the team reflects on how to become more effective, then tunes and adjusts its behavior accordingly.*"

[25] abid. Principle: "*Our highest priority is to satisfy the customer through early and continuous delivery of valuable software.*"

[26] abid. Principle: "*Working software is the primary measure of progress.*"

[27] C.R. Jakobsen, project manager at the CMMI level-5 certified company Systematic in Denmark, reports this benefit in J. Sutherland, C.R. Jakobsen, and K. Johnson, "Scrum and CMMI Level 5: The Magic Potion for Code Warriors," *Proceedings of the Agile 2007 Conference* (Washington, D.C., 2007), p. 273. Also online at http://jeffsutherland.com/scrum/Sutherland-ScrumCMMI6pages.pdf.

benefits. Yet, Carsten Ruseng Jakobsen believes that, "However if you carefully combine them you get a strong combination of needed discipline and agile values and techniques, that can be adjusted to the degree of interaction the customer is offering. In short I believe that both CMMI and Lean/Agile is good, but the combination of the two is even better." [28]

Thus, on a global project you can leverage CMMI in order to know what kind of processes to establish. And for ensuring a valuable relationship with your outsourced team, an agile approach provides recommendations (e.g. by the value system and the principles of the Agile Manifesto) how these processes should be established. Bill McMichael, Director of quality assurance of Primavera Systems, describes how his company took advantage of being ISO 9001-certified when establishing an offshore development center: "The procedure documentation that had been written proved to be invaluable in helping to communicate and ramp up the new team members on Primavera's implementation of Scrum. ... The teams were actually surprised by the degree of change, and so the documents again proved valuable as validation of the evolution of the development processes – serving as benchmark of Primavera's continual improvement efforts."[29]

The most important notion for harmonizing methodologies is that they share the same value system and, based on that, come up with practices (the details of which can differ from team to team) that support the same values. The problem is that sharing the same value system requires the transfer of tacit knowledge, which is much harder than the transfer of explicit knowledge.

Equal Rights

Every team member should receive the same education. I emphasize this, because I've seen too often that only the member of the main site received the required education. That education shouldn't only cover the necessary skills for developing the system, but also knowledge about the process in place. Ensure that all team members will be trained in agile processes on their project. Depending on project size, organize training at every site or bring together team members at one site to train. If

---

[28] Carsten Ruseng Jakobsen: private conversation.

[29] B. McMichael and M. Lombardi, "ISO 9001 and Agile Development" *Proceedings of the Agile 2007 Conference* (Washington, D.C., 2007), p. 264.

practical, the latter also benefits team members by providing another opportunity to get to know each other.

Depending on individuals' prior experience with agile processes, I recommend assigning an experienced (as far as possible internal) coach to every team, or at least every site. If you can only afford one experienced agile coach for a whole project, ask him or her to travel continuously from site to site to ensure all team members are on the same page regarding the development process.[30] Conducting these training courses and hiring experienced coaches are both expensive undertakings, but project success depends upon budgeting for those costs.

9.4 Summary

Distributed teams benefit from following agile practices. Although collocated teams can use those practices right away, it is more difficult to do so for dispersed teams. For instance, a heavily dispersed team typically has difficulties using pair programming. However, if dispersed team members work in approximately the same time zone and come together in-person frequently, virtual pair programming can be beneficial. Refactoring can be problematic if not everyone on the team pays attention to it all the time. The major difficulty is that an ignored refactoring can easily spread from being a feature-team issue to a project-wide issue, which is much harder to coordinate. Therefore, the best solution is to conduct a refactoring as soon as the need is detected, before it becomes a global issue. Especially if a feature team lacks the proximity of its product owner, it can communicate features via acceptance tests, a practice that helps avoid misunderstandings in the requirement specification because tests are precise, unambiguous, and especially executable. This practice also enables the feature team to test whether it understands the requirements correctly. However, it is always better to have the product owner collocated with the feature team and to use acceptance tests as an add-on to the product owner's direct support.

If a team has problems applying an agile practice, it should give the proven practice a serious try before examining the objec-

---

[30]For detailed information on agile coaching, see R. Davies and L. Sedley, *Agile Coaching* (Raleigh, NC: Pragmatic Bookshelf, 2009)

tives of the practice and then coming up with other practices that aim for the same objectives as the problematic practice.

Synchronizing within a team, across teams, and across sites is essential in order to ensure that every project member seeks the same objectives. Especially feature teams that are dispersed need to synchronize daily. As Carmel points out, "When a remote site does not fully understand project status, it will end up making faulty decisions with partial and incorrect information. Additionally, the remote site may feel emotionally left out and conspiracy theories will emerge."[31]

The closer people are to one another, the easier it is to organize daily synchronization. The greater the distance between people, the more creative they need to be to balance the organizational overhead with the effectiveness of the meeting. It is often helpful to switch modes, technologies, times, and the like, in order to better ensure mutual respect among everyone involved. Although time difference typically is viewed as a big constraint, it can be a means toward team bonding, as Allsop reports, "With time differences you generally have to develop a good relationship with team members because you continually call on each other to make small sacrifices, like taking a call outside working hours. This bleed into your social time seems to catalyze a bleed from your working life into your social life, blurring the lines between the two."[32]

If several teams work on the same product, it is very helpful if they agree to the same development culture. However, it is not only important to come up with rules, guidelines, and patterns, but as well to ensure that knowledge gained during the project is well spread. Furthermore, teams periodically must check that the agreements they've reached are still valid and helpful. If not, they have to be changed, omitted, or provided with more support in order to be implemented. Although defining such a culture jointly is very important, it is also important to allow the different teams some differences in implementation detail. Teams need not be forced to follow exactly the same approach as long as they do not put the work of other feature teams at risk.

---

[31] E. Carmel,, op. cit., p. 105.

[32] Thanks to Jamie Allsop for sharing this insight.

10. Introducing Agility to Distributed Projects

Small steps are better than no steps.

— Willy Brandt

Introducing an agile process even at the start of a distributed project requires special attention to ensure that the whole project shares the same agile values. A good strategy is to begin with a small, starting team, and then grow the group slowly and smoothly over different sites, but getting in at the beginning is not always feasible. A bigger challenge is to introduce agile processes into an existing project requiring the focus on creating awareness of and contribution to process change from every site involved.[1] Possible approaches include introducing change one team at a time, or undertaking process change project-wide.

Both agile and global strategies amplify pitfalls for and problems of software development and organizations. In fact, many teams are reluctant to implement agile processes or to believe in the opportunities global projects present because they mistakenly blame inherent problems of software development or the organization itself on agile and/or global circumstances. As Ebert points out, "Outsourcing and offshoring of software development can improve your ability to compete and your productivity. Yet, they show your problems rigorously and amplify them. In general, the problems had been there before!"[2] Like global development are agile processes known for making existing problems transparent. Retrospectives provide a practical way for teams to identify specific issues, and determine whether these issues are *caused* by agile or global processes (which would be bad, and is rarely happening) or *made transparent* by

---

[1] For detailed information about how to communicate change, see: Naomi Karten: *Changing how you Manage and Communicate Change. Focusing on the human side of change.* IT Governance Publishing, 2009

[2] C. Ebert, *Outsourcing kompakt,* op. cit., p. 105.

them (which is good, because only if we know about our existing issues can we solve them). This distinction helps to address the root cause of the problem.

10.1 Start Locally, Grow Globally

In my experience, the most-effective way to introduce agile processes and infuse shared culture—at the beginning of a project—is to introduce techniques to one team, starting locally at one site, and then growing it organically to multiple sites. Starting with one local team creates not only the base of the system, as for example the integration and build mechanism, but the development culture as well. A different but frequently effective method used to initiate process change centers on bringing members of one originally dispersed team together at one location, and then sending them back to their separate sites to share what they learn.

Depending on project complexity, you might need three iterations or more for getting started. However, I would never allow more time than three months for the whole starting phase, giving project members what I believe is sufficient time to set up the environment, provide the core for further development, and familiarize themselves with agile methods as they apply to distributed projects but not enough time for people to try to perfect everything. In using this time-boxed approach, I am reminded of a wisdom attributed to Winston Churchill: "*Perfection* is spelled P-A-R-A-L-Y-S-I-S."

So, it is better to not prolong this time-boxed initial phase but rather to stop after the defined timeframe and then start building up the whole team. As previously noted, part of forming the starting team is to establish the development culture for the whole distributed project. No matter if organized to work on project process, infrastructure, technology, or the initial system, the starting team's task is to start development, not to complete it. This is important, because you can't anticipate everything that will be needed later on (neither for the process nor for the software) anyway. The starting team also trains to internalize one, shared, agile philosophy. Imparting this philosophy slowly to all teams, in order to spread it outward, goes far to help ensure continuity and strengthen project-wide communication. Clearly, it is harder to start off right, from the beginning, with several distributed teams than to bring in the distribution as well as raise the number of teams when there is already something in place that can be evolved.

Collocation and Rotation

I always try to bring members of a starting team together at one location. This doesn't mean that the starting team members are all based at this location but that people from every location meet in person at that location. This way, each site influences the basis of the project and cultivates ownership of all project essentials, establishing understanding and mutual respect among all sites. In my experience, when starting team members all come from one physical site, people from other sites usually do not respond well to or integrate values imposed on them.

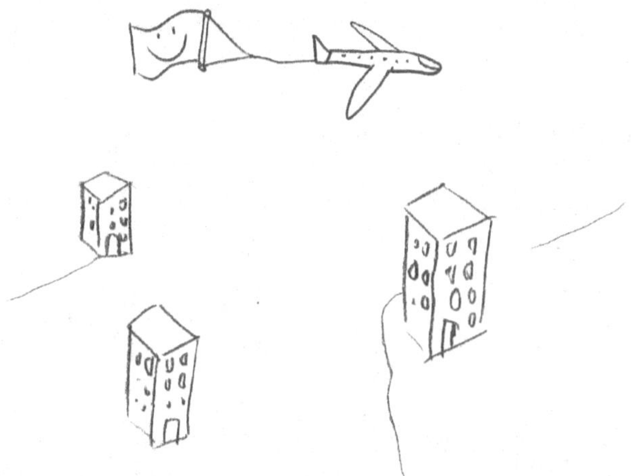

Collocation and Rotation

It is very difficult to start a project if dispersed starting-team members do not meet in person. I'm not suggesting that project failure is inevitable in such a case, simply that establishing a solid, strong basis is much more difficult and will require more time (and is therefore more expensive) than bringing together starting team members first at one location and then at rotating locations while participants prepare and plan for a project. If you time-box the starting phase to for example six iterations, you should put the starting team in a position so that it can work in turn at the different locations during that timeframe. For instance the starting team might work the first two iterations at a US-based site, the next two at a European site and the last two iterations at an Indian site. Getting started at all sites involved right from the beginning will help establishing a good relationship between all the sites. Splitting the start-up phase across different sites has additional implications:

- *Loss of time:* Travel costs not only money but also time. Additionally, starting-team members may feel daunted or discouraged by having to start over, in many senses, every time they change location, finding it difficult to tie in seamlessly with the status achieved at the last site.
- *Profit in time:* Pre-work conducted at different sites prepares team members and project managers for the future reality of a project. The sooner people identify difficulties of coordination at specific sites, the better, and their effort costs less time than later on when dispersed development is considerably more complicated.

Fundamental Iterations

Any project requires some pre-work, even if only to gather information in order to plan. For instance, team members may have to learn about a business domain, they may want to explore different technical possibilities and set up, say, a configuration-management or build-server infrastructure before they actually start working. The agile DSDM method terms this pre-work phase "foundations," and defines it as a period that "establishes firm and enduring foundations for the project. The three essential perspectives of business, solution and management are combined to provide a robust and flexible project focus."[3]

I think of this starting phase in terms of fundamental iterations: Although not focused on development, a team can still structure information-gathering and planning in an iteration. In Scrum, this concept is called Sprint Zero or Exploration Sprint—the ground-laying work before starting development, when the real sprints start. Iterations during the project start have an iteration

---

[3]For the Dynamic Systems Development method (DSDM), see: http://www.dsdm.org/atern/lifecycle/foundations/ (registration is required, but it's *free*).

goal, work to be estimated, and, at the end of an iteration, accomplishments to be measured (and celebrated). The iteration goals can include classifying and estimating key user stories, exploring possible architectures, or even estimating potential risks.

Typically, agile projects conclude the starting phase with a first release. Thus, the project start is not only one or a sequence of iterations, but also serves as a dry run for a bigger goal. Hubert Smits reports from his experience on a global project spread between the USA, France and Israel, where the lead product owner came up with a release plan starting with the following objectives for the first release: "Proof of architecture through minimal business functionality, reducing technology risks." [4]

By structuring the base work in line with early iterations, project members can restrict work and time on pre-development tasks. Of course, some of these tasks typically threaten to extend into development, refusing to be completed (done-done) until the end of the project. Team members could possibly spend the whole lifetime of a project in the starting phase, which is why it is important early on to define a timeframe.

Time and again, I have seen that, without benefit of a solid agile process during the starting phase, projects stall and do not progress smoothly. These projects often lose about half of the project's development time while setting everything up. Yet, iterations are a great means to also organize non-development tasks. The major objective of the starting phase is to set up a development environment enough for people to start working. Using a result-driven agile process is, to my way of thinking, a great way for getting these preparation tasks done in a timely manner although some infrastructure work and other preparatory tasks will also need to be performed during later iterations and, most probably, throughout an entire project.

Early-On Iteration

By practicing with time-boxed iterations with well-defined iteration goals during the project start, teams experience how it feels to structure work in iterations and benefit from getting used to the agile process early on. Possible iteration goals

---

[4] Hubert Smits. Implementing Scrum in a Distributed Software Development Organization. Course material for Agile 2007. (Quote from p.2)

for the fundamental iterations are the compilation of a 'Hello World' in the specific project environment, the presentation of a spike (or prototype) for a specific technical problem, or showing an example acceptance test in the project's test environment. All iterations—including the fundamental ones—should follow a plan-do-inspect-adapt cycle in which the following are performed:

- Split iteration goals into coarse-grained features, and those in turn into tasks.
- Estimate features and tasks and then commit to actual delivery that will be presented and measured at the end of the iteration.
- Use the iteration review to inspect iteration achievements and retrospective findings to make necessary changes to the process.

Iterating work from the start of a project also helps teams make mistakes earlier, when they presumably are easier to fix. For example, solving initial integration-and-build problems across several sites will prevent failures of complex tasks and loss of work later on. In an interview conducted by Philip Armour, Aginity CEO Doug Grimsted explains the benefit: "Its purpose is to generate the 'Omigosh!' realizations, but to do it early and in a controlled way. Then we don't get the omigosh late and in the final product where we can't manage the consequences."[5] Regard early iterations as an investment in terms of being failure-intense. Take the opportunity as a team to start learning as early as possible.

Time-Boxed Project Start

One difficulty is figuring out the actual point at which pre-work is finished—and, if you ask any member of the starting team, you will always hear that there is unfinished work. Although this is probably true, set priorities right directly at the beginning in order not to lose the project's lifetime to endless planning and pre-work.

Time-boxed iterations are steered by priorities that will provide the highest business value for the project. Even if there is work

---

[5] P.G. Armour, op. cit., p. 15.

left at the end of the timeframe, the starting team will have worked on the most important tasks before starting the "real" project, which includes growing the team.

10.2 Growing Teams and Growing Sites

If your project is a rather large one, then after completing fundamental iterations, most projects expand manpower, adding more people to the project. Adding more people will not only help to scale up the number of teams but also the number of sites. As development work begins, projects integrate new team members, ensuring that project culture spreads across all teams and sites.

Kick-Off

Shifting from project start to real development is an excellent opportunity to bring the whole project (or dispersed team members) together so that everyone invests in project goals and approach. This kick-off event marks project members' first joint experience in bridging distance and working together efficiently, as Kobayashi-Hillary points out: "Efficiency often improves dramatically when you work with someone you have met in person, even if there is no specific reason to meet." [6]

The kick-off helps team members get to know each other, and serves as a training venue for project processes. Very often, projects plan the first release, the first iteration, and clarify open issues at the kick-off, as Hubert Smits reports: "All team members were flown into Tel Aviv to participate in training and planning. The structure of the training was received enthusiastically by all participants, and all participants used the time together well to create a team spirit, bond and work through many questions and issues." [7]

---

[6] Mark Kobayashi-Hillary. A passage to India. ACM Queue. February 2005. p. 54-60 (quote on p. 59)

[7] Hubert Smits. Implementing Scrum in a Distributed Software Development Organization. Course material for Agile 2007. (Quote from p.2).

Kick-off

Combining the kick-off with training also provides the happy side effect that project team members develop relationships and bonds. My projects have benefited by starting the kick-off with a simulation such as Extreme Construction, which gives everyone a feel for what it will be like to work with agile methods.[8] We simultaneously work on overcoming communication barriers. Addressing issues that informal kick-off activities help to alleviate, Fowler reports on his experiences working with teams from Asia: "... people are often discouraged from asking questions, talking about problems, warning about unfeasible deadlines, or proposing alternatives to perceived instructions from superiors."[9]

With their focus on playful simulations, people tend to forget they are learning agile methods and about their new environment, and engage in the simulation. Typically, project members create experiences and memories together that later smooth the way for voicing concerns as well as objectives.

---

[8] For Extreme Hour, see: http://c2.com/xp/ExtremeHour.html. Also see Planning Game: http://csis.pace.edu/~bergin/xp/planninggame.html and Extreme Construction: http://csis.pace.edu/\~bergin/extremeconstruction/.

[9] M. Fowler, op. cit.

Project-Culture Transmittal

Growing a team takes cultivation of team ethos and spirit—the project culture. Agile projects sometimes benefit from creating a role colleagues and I call "foster parents."[10] Foster parents are responsible for supporting a feature team in every way possible. They ensure that the new team understands project process, technology and infrastructure, guidelines and patterns (such as coding standards and architecture). Furthermore, foster parents help their team improve and propagate project culture, communicating suggestions and concerns to management, and helping grow team relationships.

Foster parents either can help and support a feature team, or (perhaps more effective) actually be part of a team. The latter implies that the starting team (whose members are generally the best foster-parent candidates) will dissolve, releasing its members to join a new feature team as foster parents. On some of my projects, we do this only partially, by just having a few starting-team members form new feature teams and other starting-team members provide support to the new feature teams while staying in their original team structure. This strategy especially makes sense if a project will want to proceed with a technical service team, for instance, responsible for improving architecture.[11]

No matter which approach a project elects, the most important factor is that it has at least one starting team member at each site to communicate project culture as set up by the starting team. The new teams should all be set up in terms of feature teams, which influences the team assembly because of the diverse skills required.

Cultural Training

Equally as important as training team members to utilize project methods and technologies and transmitting project culture is learning about each site's culture. Project-culture transmission depends upon all parties' mutual understanding. As Krishna, Sahay, and Walsham emphasize, "Cultural training is often perceived as necessary only in one direction, namely for the

---

[10]For more on foster parents, see Eckstein, op. cit., p. 208.

[11]More on technical service teams in Chapter 3 "Building Teams".

staff from the software supplier to learn about the culture of the countries of their client organization. Regardless of any ethical concerns about such a culturally-blind attitude, it is also surely bad business practice."[12]

In order to develop a truly coherent project culture, all sites must contribute. Cultural training should include basic language skills for all sites. Language schools offer not only courses to teach English but, for example, to teach various English-language accents. I learned the need for this first-hand when conducting an English-language workshop with a team in China. To determine my overall effectiveness at the end of the workshop, I asked for anonymous feedback. One comment noted, "Language point of view, good enough to make presentation. But still can improve so that you can understand our poor English in a better way."

This point is important. In truth, multiple times during the workshop, I had a hard time understanding one or another participant's Chinese-accented English. The comment brought home to me that it is up to me to improve my understanding of an accent. I see as well that English-language sentence construction constitutes an additional challenge for non-native speakers, for me a goal still to attain.

---

[12]S. Krishna, S. Sahay, and G. Walsham, op. cit., loc. cit.

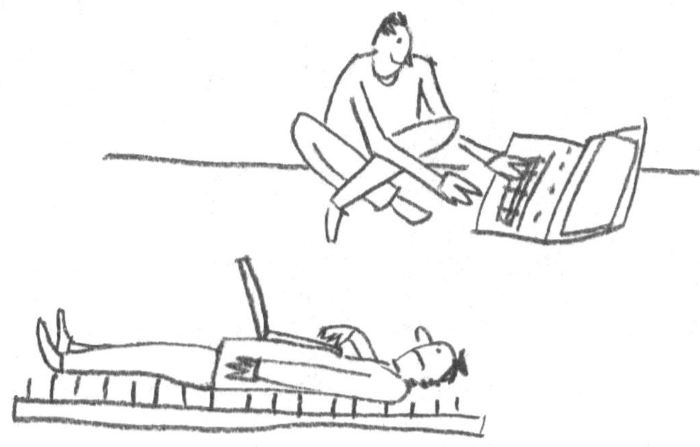

Cultural Training

Integrating New People

If the project grows again later, new members should be assigned to different, existing feature teams, rather than form one new feature team. Assigning new people this way helps spread the project culture as well as helps newcomers get acquainted with the domain, the technology, the process, and experienced team members. The existing team members will provide support for the new members to get acquainted with the project specifics. This is also a recommended strategy for including a new site. Project members belonging to this new site are then invited to become members of one of the (at least now) dispersed existing feature teams.

Relying on mentoring only, would slow down the affected feature teams extremely. Additional training will provide education about the technical, the business and the process perspective of the project. For transmitting these different perspectives we ask one of the architects, product owners and coaches to deliver the training. This training is typically a combination of classical lecture-style training and one-on-one sessions.

10.3 Introducing Agile Processes to an Existing Project

Often, developers introduce agile practices to an existing project without officially announcing a change in the software development process. Practices such as unit-test and pair programming do not significantly change the external perception of a team's behavior. However, accepting change to the whole approach is more difficult, requiring the application of the whole plan-do-inspect-adapt cycle. Such a change is likely to fail without a common, official agreement, especially because it will affect more people than just the developers. For example, to successfully implement agile methods, the product owner must steer the team through priorities and be willing to provide feedback. The most difficult change is to abandon a command-and-control approach in favor to one that invests responsibility in all team members. Some team members might be overburdened with this more responsive role and some managers might not be participatory leaders in a sense that they are not used to trust and empower their teams. With a commonly understood agreement, team members know they will not shoulder project burdens alone and unsupported, and their responsibilities and rewards will be public and negotiable.

Gradual versus Project-Wide Change

The first decision regarding introducing agile processes to an existing project is to determine whether it benefits the project more to introduce transition to one team at a time, or to all teams at all sites at once. The downside of implementing transition one team after another is that the change in process is more subtle and less uniform, which makes it easier for people to fall back into old habits, especially since other surrounding teams still follow the old methods.

Therefore, I always recommend that the whole project changes at once to the new approach. This works the best if changes are made explicit at a kick-off event—comparable in practice to the previously described kick-off event at the beginning of a project. Yet, this is not a kick-off to the project (because the project is existing), but instead a kick-off for the process change. For this kick-off, if possible bring all project members together and define the starting line for the process, taking care to clearly distinguish differences with the old approach. Agility provides a wonderful tool for this: the retrospective. Invite all team members or representatives from each team to reflect on things that work and those that need to be improved. This initial retrospective should focus on process improvement. Start this retrospective with basic agile-development training so team members have *tools* at hand (which are truly practices, principles, or attitudes) they can use for improving their process. The result of this retrospective will be a first set of reasonably actionable changes.

Team Structure Change

The biggest challenge of introducing agile methods to an existing project is change in team structure. Typically, non-agile projects structure teams by activities and/or technological skill. The decision to change to a feature-team structure requires courage and a detailed plan that garners participants' support.

One way to make the transition to a feature-team structure gradually is to keep the old, organizational-wide team structure in place and introduce feature teams virtually. People stay in their existing hierarchy, reporting to the same people, but work in different groups to deliver requested features. As long as everyone understands delivery of features as the highest priority (and not e.g. the activities which might be the basis for the old organizational team structure), this can be a successful approach. On some of my projects, we follow this approach, which provides the advantage of feature-oriented delivery but the disadvantage of duplicated organizational structure. Similar to a matrix organization this approach enables a combination of agile feature teams and traditional structures.

On most of my projects with virtual feature teams, sooner or later, a vocal majority questions our old organizational structure and it is eventually eliminated. In defense, I merely note that having this duplicated structure in place facilitates a smooth transition to real feature teams.

More and/or Better Coaches

In the middle of a project's lifetime, the project is not easily downsized to one (starting) team on which to establish new project and process culture. Instead, pains must be taken to carefully establish and transmit project culture with all teams and sites concurrently and continually. Continue the efforts of the kick-off and retrospective sessions to create awareness of change. Recruit coaches familiar with agile methods to ease transition and encourage project development progress in spite of adjusting to change. For more on recruiting coaches, review the section on equal rights in Chapter 9, "Honing Practices." Ensure that all coaches have a frequent exchange and are working together very closely. Otherwise it is likely that each coach implements a different process and thus in turn each team gains a different understanding of the agile process applied.

Estimation and Velocity

When introducing an agile process to an existing project you can normally assume that the pre-work is done and the starting phase is concluded. Some projects may want to translate original estimates to agile iterations. Other projects consider switching to an agile methodology because they are not able to determine realistic project deadlines, or whether they would be able to finish the project at all. If features are not estimated or a project's velocity is unknown, organize an estimation workshop soon after the agile transition kick-off to quantify project time and cost.

I recommend that each feature team set aside time to hold an estimation workshop during which to estimate the features it will later on develop. Reliable estimation is only possible if projects first assign feature teams to each domain area. Although estimates will differ, after about the third iteration, project members can calculate teams' velocities and relate their different estimation units, because the more optimistic team will finish fewer of their estimated features per iteration whereas the more pessimistic team will complete more of their estimated features. Additionally, the remaining features resemble the same disparity because the feature team having provided the estimate will also develop those features. If you are in the need of bringing this disparity more to equilibrium, I recommend starting the first estimation workshop with representatives from each feature team. This group of people will then provide a common baseline for the estimates and will transmit this baseline to their feature team.

If the features are already estimated (probably having used a different technique) –which is very likely for an existing project– but the velocity is unknown, I recommend using these existing estimates. The velocity of each feature team is then calculated at the end of the iteration by summing up the original estimates of the completed features. We treat the original estimates like (complexity) points independent of the initial estimation unit. The numbers will be collected from each feature team and summed up. The total will be used in turn for the overall project's velocity and as such for forecasting the remaining course of the project.

Lone Fighter

Perhaps the most contentious transition to agile methods comes when one team, which is part of a large distributed project, wants to change to an agile approach, but the rest of the project either is not aware of it or does not support the change. The first step I take is to communicate irrefutable enthusiasm and justification for agile methods as they pertain to the whole project, and then discuss specifics of the proposed process change. I note that the process in place may be a reliable one, and further observe that people justifiably fear changing to an unknown process that might not be as effective. In other words – if there is no need to change the approach, I would not recommend changing it.

However, even a case in which the current process clearly is not effective, just one individual's defensiveness and lack of support for change can stand firmly in change's way. By introducing agile development practices and by applying strategies like the adapter pattern which enables conformity to existing team interfaces, or procedures for delivering needed documents, an individual team can apply parts of an agile process.

As soon as the lone team in transition starts to steer through features and discovers it is not set up as a properly agile feature team, or requests feedback from the product owner and discovers it does not have one, or needs input from outside and cannot obtain it, real difficulties will manifest. Accordingly, although one team might be able to follow an agile approach, the full benefit of agility can not be reached without other project teams also changing their process and evolving toward an agile model. Incompatibilities of the different processes heavily burden a project and the only benefit for the lone agile team might reside in gaining experiences with agility.

Two ways to incorporate agile methods despite lack of project-wide support follow:

- *Use one team's successful transition as persuasion:* After the lone team makes the transition to an agile approach, other teams will recognize the benefits and mobilize project-wide change.
- *Use subprojects as models for change:* If the project is really not a single unified effort but an assembly of different subprojects, each (sub-) team will be responsible for its own subproject and will minimize interaction with other teams. Each team can select the process it finds most effective. The subteams can deliver their subprojects individually in case they are really independent. Of course, if a single delivery of all subprojects is required at the end, beware of the "big bang" integration at the project's end that can threaten everyone's progress (and that wouldn't be required if all subteams would follow an agile approach).

10.4 Summary

Introducing agile iterations at the beginning of a project not only establishes a rhythm of process and progress but also reinforces focus on delivering the highest possible business value throughout a project. During the pre-work phase, iterations structure preparation and help a project stay within a pre-defined timeframe. I recommend one iteration as an ideal timeframe for the starting phase and three months as a maximum timeframe, depending on the project's complexity. A pre-defined timeframe reduces the risk of spending too much time planning and preparing.

Begin with one (small) team only and propagate agile process through this starting team, which optimally should be collocated, although –and this is actually preferred– individual members do not have to be based originally at the same location. Let starting-team members work for, say, an iteration at each future site.

When growing the team, ask members of the starting team to serve as foster parents to the new teams. In this role, they can not only support new team members technically, but also culturally, thereby helping them to get acquainted with the project culture.

If the project is already underway, it is helpful to assign coaches to enable the different teams to get up to speed with the new approach. It is easier if the whole project switches at once to the new process. This switch is best initiated by a process kick-off event that brings the whole team together.

11. Afterword

There is nothing in a different human being
That is not in me.
This is the only foundation
For the understanding among all human beings.

– Erich Fromm

Today, it is expected of all projects to react flexibly in order to increase value for the customer. Actually, this is more than an expectation. As Clarence Darrow observed,

> It is not the strongest of the species that survive, nor the most intelligent, but the ones most responsive to change.

Software development projects must exercise flexibility in order to increase product value. To successfully deliver a product, individual team members as well as the organization itself must actively respond to change—in other words, maintain agility. Issues I address in this book are issues that every project needs to address, no matter if applying an agile process or not. Agility forces projects to actually face challenges right away, never leaving it an option to ignore these issues. If some of my recommendations seem little more than common sense, keep the wisdom in the following in mind, "Common sense isn't common." It is fact that people are often remarkably shortsighted, blind even, when facing risks and dangers that are clearly evident.

If this book leaves some questions in the minds of some readers, I hope that it has provided enough material on all possible challenges a global project could face so as to help readers develop solutions for specific situations and settings. The root of our software development troubles and successes may be that we are all human, but just possibly our projects' salvation resides in our ability to harness creativity and courage to always look for a better way to accomplish them successfully.

Whenever people start talking about global software development, one of the first topics that comes up is cultural differences and how to overcome them. I have realized over the course of many global projects that the biggest advantage of global teams is, in fact, the diversity of team members. We can benefit greatly from a distributed project environment, appreciating the diversity of people as it guarantees that we gain different insights from different perspectives. To strengthen our processes and relationships, we can focus not on team members' differences but on similarities -and there are more of them as we all might think at the beginning- because in the end we are all humans.

Glossary

Ambassador:

A project member who represents his or her home site at a different site, and ensures that communication flows back and forth between sites.

Asynchronous communication:

Any communication setting or format that incorporates a time delay in participants' conversation (for example, e-mail).

Chief architect:

A project member whose main responsibility is to ensure conceptual integrity and the big picture (technically), and to ensure these are understood by every team member.

Chief product owner:

See: *Lead product owner.* See also: *Product owner.*

Collaboration platform:

Platform that allows sharing artifacts among a dispersed group. More sophisticated collaboration platforms allow also changing the common artifacts. An example for a collaboration platform is a wiki.

Communication and trust threshold:

See: *Threshold for trusted connections.*

Complexity point:

See: *Feature point.*

Conceptual integrity:

The correlation of a system's strategy, philosophy, and techniques (for example, the look and feel of a system should be consistent for every application).

Continuous integration:

The whole system undergoes integration-and-build whenever a team member completes a development task.

Daily build:

A build of an entire system performed once a day.

Daily Scrum:

See: *Daily synchronization.*

Daily synchronization:

A team synchronization performed once a day, the purpose of which is for every team member to gain the same understanding about the status of the project. (Also known in Scrum as a "Daily Scrum," and in XP as a "Stand-Up Meeting.")

Developer:

Any feature-team member needed to deliver a feature (for example, a designer, tester, programmer, documenter, or user interface specialist).

Direct communication:

Face-to-face communication. See also: *In-person meeting*.

Dispersed team:

Members constituting one team while located at different locations.

Distributed teams:

Different teams (not team members) working on the same project while located at different sites.

Domain team:

See: *Feature team*.

Done-done:

A feature that is ready for delivery. The individual steps to achieve this status vary for every project. Typically, to achieve the done-done state, a feature must be analyzed, designed, implemented, tested, integrated, reviewed, documented, and deployed (the order of these steps might also vary).

Expatriate:

A project member working for a long period of time at a site or sites other than the home location.

External release:

A system's outcome that is used in production by the customer. See also: *Internal release, Release*.

Feature:

Stakeholder-requested business functionality. Also known as "user story," "use case," or "business requirement."

Feature point:

Estimation unit for a feature that accounts for its relative complexity compared to other features.

Feature team:

A group of people that work together to deliver business functionality.

Follow the sun:

The turn-over of the development effort between the sites follows (physically) the sun. This way at all times during a 24 hours day somebody will work on the system in his day time.

Fundamental iteration(s):

The "pre-work" a team performs before initiating development, including establishing an environment that will support development (for example, information gathering, iteration planning, and estimation) such that the team(s) can start working. (Also known in Scrum as a "Sprint Zero," "Exploration Sprint," and in DSDM as a "Foundations.")

Heartbeat retrospective:

A retrospective conducted in the same rhythm as the heartbeat of the project—at the end of each iteration.

Ideal time:

The time available in terms of working hours without any interruptions. See also: *Real time* (complement).

Individual feature-team retrospective:

A retrospective conducted by members of a single feature team.

In-person meeting:

Meeting or conversation that takes place face-to-face. See also: *Direct communication*.

Internal release:

A system's outcome that goes through the same steps as an external release, but is *not* used in production by the customer. See also: *External release, Release*.

Iteration:

A time-boxed development cycle with development and delivery focused on features, typically enduring two weeks, at the end of which the team delivers the newly built system.

Joint-site retrospective:

A retrospective conducted by all project members, from different teams, working at one location.

Lead product owner:

A person who steers the team of product owners and maintains communication with the customer throughout the project, ensuring that the system is coherent in connection with the customer's business activities and that the different feature teams are always working on features with the highest priorities. See also: *Chief product owner, Product owner*.

Offshoring:

The execution of business activities outside the home country of the organization, which may be performed by a subsidiary of the same organization (residing in a different country) or a different organization.

Onsite customer:

See: *Product owner.*

Outsourcing:

A contractual relationship wherein one company hires another to perform management and/or business activities.

Planning Poker:

An estimation technique—centered around team estimation, estimation of complexity (not time or duration), and relative estimates—in which team members individually assign point scores to features, and then reveal their "hands," discussing scores and reconciling differences of opinion.

Pre-planning meeting:

A meeting to plan the upcoming iteration, which is steered by the chief product owner and includes the team of product owners and architect(s), with the goal of discovering possible dependencies between features.

Product owner:

A representative of the customer who serves as customer liaison to a feature team, decides requirements priorities, ensures that the system under development maintains the highest possible business value, and ensures the functional coherence of the product. On large projects, there is typically a team of product owners, where each product owner assumes the role of the customer for a single feature team. See also: *Chief product owner.*

Project-Wide retrospective:

Depending on the size of the project, a retrospective that is conducted either with all project members or with representatives from each feature team.

Project-Wide synchronization:

Similar to a daily synchronization, a project-wide synchronization's purpose is the usually daily synchronization between different subteams, each of which sends a representative to report on what his or her team is working (and especially what each is struggling with) at that time, thereby exchanging status of the big picture across the whole project. See also: *Scrum of Scrums*.

Realistic planning:

A planning activity that schedules only as much as can reasonably be achieved based on estimates from previous iterations. See also: *Retrospective*.

Real time:

A quantification of estimated time available, after deducting the time that it takes to address all interruptions (for example, answering e-mails, the phone, or questions from peers). See also: *Ideal time* (complement).

Refactoring:

Improving the internal structure of the code without changing the external behavior.

Release:

A time-boxed development cycle, typically lasting about three months, which is completed with the deployment of a new version of the product, with the development and deployment effort organized by groups of features that fulfill customer requirements.

Release retrospective:

A retrospective that is conducted after a release. See also: *Retrospective.*

Retrospective:

Reflection on and analysis of development efforts and results that support continuous learning. Participants reflect on what worked and what didn't work during a specific timeframe of development, and share ideas about what and how to change during a specific future timeframe.

Satellite:

A site whose team members assist communication between distant sites and bridge a large time difference between those distant sites (for example, a site in Europe can serve as a satellite situated between sites in Asia and on the West Coast of the United States).

Scrum of Scrums:

See: *Project-wide synchronization.*

Site Scrum of Scrums:

The Site Scrum of Scrums' purpose is the synchronization between different subteams, which are all located at the same site. The procedure is similar to the Scrum of Scrums, yet with the site related activities in focus. See also: *Scrum of Scrums.*

Smart meeting:

A pre-scheduled, regular meeting that may or may not take place depending on whether people deem meeting necessary or not.

Smell:

Hint or evidence to a problem.

Subteam:

A team formed by splitting a large team into several smaller groups, each of which typically comprises ten or fewer people.

Synchronous communication:

A communication setting or format that forces participants to converse and respond in real time (for example, the telephone). See also: *Asynchronous communication.*

Threshold for trusted connection:

The point at which two people or groups of people typically lose respect for and/or trust in one another if their relationship has not been nurtured and re-established, for example, by in-person meetings scheduled no less frequently than every eight-to-twelve weeks. See also: *In-person meeting.*

References

Articles

Ambler, S. "Bridging the Distance," *Dr. Dobb's Portal,* (August 2002). Online: http://www.ddj.com/dept/architect/184414899.

Armour, P.G. "Agile...and Offshore: An Interview with a New Paradigm," *Communications of the ACM,* Vol. 50, No. 1 (January 2007), pp. 13-16.

Bekkering, E., and J.P. Shim. "Trust in Videoconferencing," *Communications of the ACM,* Vol. 49, No. 7 (July 2006), pp. 103-7.

Biehl, M. "Success Factors for Implementing Global Information Systems," *Communications of the ACM,* Vol. 50, No. 1 (January 2007), pp. 53-58.

Braithwaite, K. and T. Joyce. "XP Expanded: Distributed Extreme Programming," *Proceedings of XP 2005* (Sheffield, Eng., 2005). pp. 180-188

Carmel, E., and P. Abbott. "Why 'Nearshore' Means That Distance Matters," *Communications of the ACM,* Vol. 50, No. 10 (October 2007), pp. 40-46.

Damian, D. "Stakeholders in Global Requirements Engineering: Lessons Learned from Practice," *IEEE Software,* (March/April, 2007), pp. 21-27.

Estublier, J. "Software Configuration Management: A Roadmap," *Proceedings of the Conference on the Future of Software Engineering* (Limerick, Ire., 2000), pp. 279-99.

Fowler, M. "Using an Agile Software Process with Offshore Development" (July 18, 2006). Online: http://martinfowler.com/articles/agileOffshore.html.

Handy, C. "Trust and the Virtual Organization," *Harvard Business Review,* Vol. 73, No. 3 (1995), pp. 40-50.

Herbsleb, D., and A. Mockus. "An Empirical Study of Speed and Communication in Globally Distributed Software Development,"

IEEE Transactions on Software Engineering, Vol. 29, No. 6 (June 2003), pp. 481-94.

Highsmith, J.A., III. "Project Management at the Edge" *in: The IT Project Leader* (February 2000), Online: http://www.jimhighsmith.com/articles/PMEdge.pdf.

Hofstede, G. and G.J. Hofstede. „Cultures and Orgainzations: Software of the Mind," *McGraw-Hill,* 2. edition. 2004

Hussman, D. "Offshore Agile Software Development," *Proceedings of XP 2005* (Sheffield, Eng., 2005).

Hvatum, L.B. "Agile Practices and Distributed Teams," *Cutter IT Journal,* Vol. 20, No. 5 (May 2007), pp. 6-11.

Jepsen, O. "Agile Meets Offshore: How Can Agile Practices Help in Offshore Projects?" *Proceedings of Agile 2006 Conference* (Minneapolis, Minn., July 2006).

Kircher, M., P. Jain, A. Corsaro, and D.L. Levine. "Distributed eXtreme Programming," *Proceedings of XP 2001* (Villasimius, Sardinia, Italy), pp. 66-71.

Kircher, M., and D.L. Levine. "The XP of TAO: Extreme Programming of Large, Open-Source Frameworks," *Proceedings of XP 2000* (Cagliari, Sardinia, Italy), pp. 463-86. Online: https://tinyurl.com/XPofTAO.

Kobayashi-Hillary, M. "A Passage to India," *ACM Queue* (February 2005), pp. 54-60.

Koh, B.J., Y.-G. Kim, B. Butler, and G.-W. Bock. "Encouraging Participation in Virtual Communities," *Communications of the ACM,* Vol. 50, No. 2 (February 2007), pp. 69-73.

Konana, P. "Can Indian Software Firms Compete with the Global Giants?" *IEEE Computer* (July 2006), pp. 43-47.

Krishna, S., S. Sahay, and G. Walsham. "Managing Cross-Cultural Issues in Global Software Outsourcing," *Communications of the ACM,* Vol. 47, No. 4 (April 2004), pp. 62-66.

McConnell, S. "Best Practices: Daily Build and Smoke Tests," *IEEE Software,* Vol. 13, No. 4 (July 1996), pp. 143-44.

McKinney, V.R., and M.M. Whiteside. "Maintaining Distributed Relationships," *Communications of the ACM*, Vol. 49, No. 3 (March 2006), pp. 82-86.

McMichael, B., and M. Lombardi. "ISO 9001 and Agile Development," *Proceedings of Agile 2007 Conference* (Washington, D.C., 2007), pp. 262-65.

Nessier, R. "Go Global! Translate the Proven Benefits of Agile Development to a Distributed Team Environment," *Agile Development* magazine (Spring 2007), pp. 7-10. Online: http://www.agilealliance.org/agile_magazines.

Pelrine, J. "Anatomy of a Scrum Project." Online: http://www.controlchaos.com/module/practicing_pelrine.pdf.

Pugh, K. "Managing Distributed and Global Teams," *Proceedings of Software Best Practices Conference* (Boston, 2007).

Sakthivel, S. "Managing Risk in Offshore Systems Development," *Communications of the ACM,* Vol. 50, No. 4 (April 2007), pp. 69-75.

Sandberg, J.-E., and L.A. Skår. "Can Agile Practices Deliver High-Quality, Large-Scale Offshored Projects?" *Proceedings of XP 2007 Conference* (Como, Italy, 2007).

Shao, B.B.M., and J.S. David. "The Impact of Offshore Outsourcing on IT Workers in Developed Countries," *Communications of the ACM,* Vol. 50, No. 2 (February 2007), pp. 89-94.

Simon, M. "Internationally Agile," *Informit.com* (March 2002). Online: http://www.informit.com/articles/article.asp?p=25929.

Smits, H. "Implementing Scrum in a Distributed Software Development Organization," *Proceedings of Agile 2007* (Washington, D.C., 2007).

Sutherland, J., C.R. Jakobsen, and K. Johnson. "Scrum and CMMI Level 5: The Magic Potion for Code Warriors," *Proceedings of Agile 2007* (Washington, D.C., 2007), pp. 272-77. Online: https://bit.ly/3tng5F1.

Tuckman, B. "Developmental Sequence in Small Groups," *Psychological Bulletin,* Vol. 63 (1965), pp. 384-89.

Books

Allen, T. *Managing the Flow of Technology: Technology Transfer and the Dissemination of Technological Information within the R&D Organization.* Cambridge, Mass.: MIT Press, 1984.

Baumeister, H., M. Marchesi and M. Holcombe (Eds.). *Extreme Programming & Agile Processes in Software-Engineering*. Berlin, Heidelberg: Springer-Verlag 2005

Beck, K., and M. Fowler. *Planning Extreme Programming*. Reading, Mass.: Addison-Wesley, 2001.

Brooks, F.P., Jr. *The Mythical Man-Month: Essays on Software Engineering*. 20th anniv. ed. Reading, Mass.: Addison-Wesley, 1995.

Carmel, E. *Global Software Teams: Collaborating Across Borders and Time Zones*. Englewood Cliffs, N.J.: Prentice-Hall, 1999.

———, and P. Tjia. *Offshoring Information Technology: Sourcing and Outsourcing to a Global Workforce*. Cambridge, Eng.: Cambridge University Press, 2005.

Cockburn, A. *Agile Software Development: The Cooperative Game*. 2nd ed. Boston: Addison-Wesley, 2006.

Cohn, M. *Agile Estimating and Planning*. Englewood Cliffs, N.J.: Prentice-Hall, 2006.

Coplien, J.O., and N.B. Harrison. *Organizational Patterns of Agile Software Development*. Englewood Cliffs, N.J.: Prentice-Hall, 2004.

Corbett, M.F. *The Outsourcing Revolution: Why It Makes Sense and How to Do It Right*. New York: Kaplan Business, 2004.

Davies, R. and Sedley, L., *Agile Coaching* Raleigh, NC: Pragmatic Bookshelf, 2009.

Derby, E., and D. Larsen. *Agile Retrospectives: Making Good Teams Great*. Raleigh, N.C.: Pragmatic Programmers, 2006.

Ebert, C. *Outsourcing kompakt: Entscheidungskriterien und Praxistipps für Outsourcing und Offshoring von Software- Entwicklung*. Amsterdam: Spektrum Akademischer Verlag/Elsevier, 2006.

Eckstein, J. *Agile Software Development in the Large*. New York: Dorset House Publishing, 2004.

Friedman, T.L. *The World Is Flat: A Brief History of the Twenty-First Century*. New York: Farrar, Straus, and Giroux, 2006.

Gabriel, R. P. *Writers' Workshops and the Work of Making Things*. Reading, Mass.: Addison-Wesley, 2002

Highsmith, J.A., III. *Agile Software Development Ecosystems.* Reading, Mass.: Addison-Wesley, 2002.

Karolak, D.W. *Global Software Development: Managing Virtual Teams and Environments.* Los Alamitos, Calif.: IEEE Computer Society Press, 1998.

Karten, N. *Changing how you Manage and Communicate Change. Focusing on the human side of change.* Camridgeshire, UK: IT Governance Publishing, 2009.

Kerth, N.L. *Project Retrospectives: A Handbook for Team Reviews.* New York: Dorset House Publishing, 2001.

Lacity, M.C., and L.P. Willcocks. *Global Information Technology Outsourcing: In Search of Business Advantage.* Hoboken, N.J.: John Wiley & Sons, 2001.

Larman, C. *Agile and Iterative Development: A Manager's Guide.* Reading, Mass.: Addison-Wesley, 2004.

Leuf, B. and W. Cunningham: *The Wiki Way: Collaboration and Sharing on the Internet.* Reading, Mass.: Addison-Wesley, 2001

Liker, J.K. *The Toyota Way: 14 Management Principles from the World's Greatest Manufacturer.* New York: McGraw-Hill, 2004.

Manns, M.L., and L. Rising. *Fearless Change: Patterns for Introducing New Ideas.* Upper Saddle River, N.J.: Pearson Education, 2005.

Marchesi, M., G. Succi, D. Wells, and L. Williams. *Extreme Programming Perspectives.* Reading, Mass.: Addison-Wesley, 2002.

Mugridge, R., and W. Cunningham. *Fit for Developing Software: Framework for Integrated Tests.* Upper Saddle River, N.J.: Pearson Education, 2005.

Poppendieck, M. and T. Poppendieck. *Lean Software Development. An Agile Toolkit.* Reading, Mass.: Addison-Wesley, 2003.

Sangwan, R., M. Bass, N. Mullick, D.J. Paulish, and J. Kazmeier. *Global Software Development Handbook.* Boca Raton, Fla.: Auerbach, 2007.

Schwaber, K., and M. Beedle. *Agile Software Development with Scrum.* Englewood Cliffs, N.J.: Prentice-Hall, 2001.

Scott, J. *Social Network Analysis: A Handbook.* 2nd ed. Thousand Oaks, Calif.: Sage Publications, 1991.

Succi, G., and M. Marchesi. *Extreme Programming Examined.* Reading, Mass.: Addison-Wesley, 2001.

Thondavadi, N., and G. Albert. *Offshore Outsourcing: Path to New Efficiencies in IT and Business Processes.* Bloomington, Ind.: Authorhouse, 2004.

Yourdon, E. *Outsource: Competing in the Global Productivity Race.* Englewood Cliffs, N.J.: Prentice-Hall, 2005.

URLs

Agile Alliance

http://agilealliance.org

Agile Manifesto

http://agilemanifesto.org

Agile Planner

http://ase.cpsc.ucalgary.ca/ase/index.php/AgilePlanning/Home

CruiseControl

http://cruisecontrol.sourceforge.net

Dynamic Systems Development Method (DSDM)

http://dsdm.org

Extreme Construction

http://csis.pace.edu/~bergin/extremeconstruction

Extreme Hour

http://c2.com/xp/ExtremeHour.html

Extreme Programming

http://c2.com/cgi/wiki?ExtremeProgrammingRoadmap

Feature Driven Development

http://www.featuredrivendevelopment.com

FIT: Framework for Integrated Test

http://fit.c2.com

FitNesse

http://fitnesse.org

Git

http://git.or.cz

Mercurial

http://www.selenic.com/mercurial

Planning Game

http://csis.pace.edu/~bergin/xp/planninggame.html

Planning Poker

http://www.planningpoker.com

Project Planning and Tracking System (PPTS)

http://ses-ppts.sourceforge.net

Scrum

http://www.controlchaos.com

Scrum Alliance

http://scrumalliance.org

SecondLife®

http://www.secondlife.com

Skype

http://skype.org

Subversion

http://subversion.tigris.org

Trac

http://trac.edgewall.org, also agile-trac: http://www.agile-trac.org/

Wideband Delphi

http://www.stellman-greene.com/aspm/content/view/23/38

XPlanner

http://xplanner.org

Yesterday's Weather

http://c2.com/cgi/wiki?YesterdaysWeather

About Jutta Eckstein

Jutta Eckstein works as an independent coach, consultant, author and speaker. She has helped many teams and organizations worldwide to make agile transitions. She is experienced in applying agile processes within medium-sized to large, distributed mission-critical projects and has written about her experiences. She holds a M.A. Business Coaching & Change Management, a Dipl.Eng. Product-Engineering, and a B.A. in Education.

She is a member of the Agile Alliance (having served on the board of directors from 2003-2007) and a member of the program committee of many different American, Asian and European conferences, where she has also presented her work.

Stay in touch with Jutta:

- @juttaeckstein
- Jutta on Linkedin[1]
- Jutta on Xing[2]
- Jutta's homepage[3]

---

[1] https://linkedin.com/in/juttaeckstein/
[2] http://xing.com/profile/Jutta_Eckstein
[3] http://jeckstein.com

Other Books by the Author

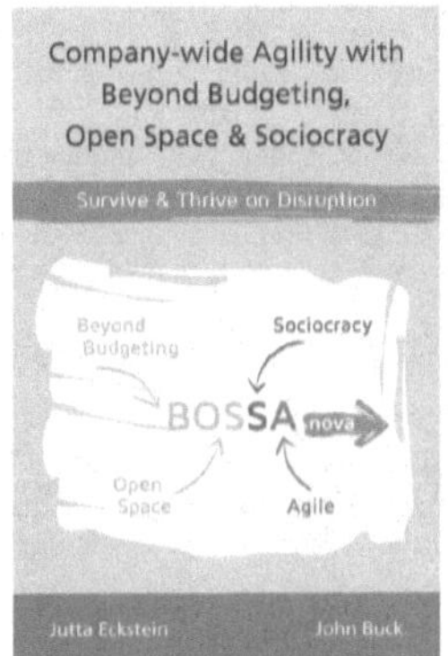

Company-wide Agility with Beyond Budgeting, Open Space & Sociocracy

Survive & Thrive on disruption

By Jutta Eckstein & John Buck

Today, companies are expected to be flexible and both rapidly responsive and resilient to change, which basically asks them to be agile. By combining Beyond Budgeting, Open Space, Sociocracy, and Agile, this book provides a practical guide for companies that want to be agile company-wide.

Enjoy insights in the book shared by Jez Humble, Diana Larsen, James Shore, Johanna Rothman, and Bjarte Bogsnes. Find out what Spotify, ING, Ericsson, and Walmart say in the book.

Quotes from early readers:

"[This is] a very important book. My hopes are that it will be the missing link between agile for teams and the flexible, adaptive and humane organisations we want to build. It's a great book. Thanks for writing it!" ~Sandy Mamoli, author of Creating Great Teams

"Just as Spotify has worked hard to make all aspects of product development align well and work together - I see Jutta and John in this book exploring methods and processes that will work very well across the whole company." ~ Anders Ivarsson, Spotify

"Company-wide Agility with Beyond Budgeting, Open Space and Sociocracy [...] makes an important case for companies to regard trust and autonomy the norm, rather than a privilege. [...] Overall a great overview of how leaders can reimagine the way power is distributed within their companies." ~ Aimee Groth, Author of The Kingdom of Happiness: Inside Tony Hsich's Zapponian Utopia

This book invites you to take a new perspective that addresses the challenges of doing business in a volatile, uncertain, complex, and ambiguous world.

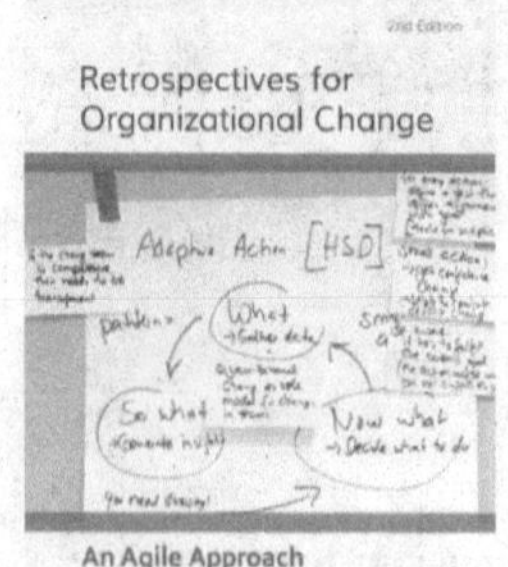

Retrospectives for Organizational Change, 2nd ed.

An Agile Approach

By Jutta Eckstein

About the book:

In this book, Jutta Eckstein examines how retrospectives —originally a kind of a facilitated workshop for gaining feedback— can be applied conceptually to initiate and implement organizational change.

Technically, retrospectives were an instrument for a group to examine a past joint period of time and learn from that. The participants of a Retrospective for Organizational Change do not share a joint past, yet they learn from their different individual experiences and use this as a basis to form a shared future. The main strength is to leverage the experiences of a diverse group. Especially if the change is dynamic, which means the approach toward the goal is unclear or if it is complex, where the goal itself is in-determinate, Retrospectives for Organizational Change can provide a way to support the change.

This book covers the conceptual idea of using Retrospectives for Organizational Change and additionally reports on the feedback and experiences of its practical application.

Linda Rising says about this book:

> "Of course, there are other books on the protocols and exercises for retrospectives, but these don't share the 'whys' of this important ritual. What Jutta has done for us is provide real experience reports that show how useful retrospectives can be and share her research around using retrospectives to lead change in an organization. Get this book and read it!"
> (Linda Rising, Co-Author of Fearless Change and More Fearless Change)

Diving for Hidden Treasures

Uncovering the Cost of Delay in Your Project Portfolio

By Johanna Rothman & Jutta Eckstein

About the book:

Does your organization value and rank projects based on estimation? Except for the shortest projects, estimation is often wrong. You don't realize the value you planned when you wanted. How can you finish projects in time to realize their potential value?

Instead of estimation, consider using cost of delay to evaluate and rank projects. Cost of delay accounts for ways projects get stuck: multitasking, other projects not releasing on time, work queuing behind experts, excessive attention to code cleanliness, and management indecision to name several.

Once you know about cost of delay, you can decide what to do about it. You can stop the multitasking. You can eliminate the need for experts. You can reduce the number of projects and features in progress. You can use cost of delay to rank projects and work in your organization. Learn to use cost of delay to make better decisions for your project, program, or project portfolio.

Have you ever wondered about how your projects become late? Are you worried that your projects become later and you don't know why?

Cost of delay can tell you where the delays occur and why. Common practices, such as multitasking, experts, and even other projects' delay can make your project late. Learn simple tools and methods for analyzing and eliminating the costs of delay in your project.

Agile Software Development in the Large

Diving into the Deep

By Jutta Eckstein

About the book:

Agile processes have revolutionized the software development industry. They're faster and more efficient than traditional software development processes. They enable developers to embrace requirement changes during the project, deliver working software in frequent iterations, and focus on the human factor in software development.

Unfortunately, agile processes are either designed for small or mid-sized software development teams or rigid frameworks are provided for large-sized teams. Yet, also large teams have to deal with rapid changes - so rigidity is not helpful for them!

With *Agile Software Development in the Large*, Jutta Eckstein—a leading speaker and consultant in the agile community—shows how to scale agile processes to teams of up to 300. The same techniques are also relevant to teams of as few as 10 developers, especially within large organizations.

Topics include:

- the agile value system as used in large teams
- the impact of a switch to agile processes
- the agile coordination of several sub-teams
- the way project size and team size influence the underlying architecture

Stop getting frustrated with inflexible processes that cripple your large endeavors! Use this book to harness the efficiency and adaptability of agile software development.

Index

A

Abbott, 62

Acceptance criteria, 34, 119, 182–184

Acceptance test, 135, 208

Action plan, 153, 160

Adams, 15

Agile Manifesto, 1, 15, 19, 21, 24, 41, 46, 52, 56, 65, 93, 113, 119, 136, 152, 165, 171, 185, 198–199

Agile methodologies, 3, 198

Agile practices, 3, 32, 58, 60, 105, 171–172, 200, 214

Agile processes, iii, 3, 65, 136, 186, 199–200, 203–204, 214

Agile software development, i–iii, 1–2, 4, 15, 25, 38–39, 77, 93, 167

Agile value system, 2, 16, 18, 152, 171

Agility, iii–2, 4–5, 7–8, 10, 12, 14–16, 18–20, 22, 32, 39, 43, 51, 55, 67, 77, 97, 106, 126, 142, 145, 152, 171, 185, 198, 203–204, 206, 208, 210, 212, 214–218, 221

Albert, 3, 93

Allsop, ii, 27, 107, 190, 201

Ambassador, 76–79, 90, 223

Ambler, 29, 74, 192

Architect, 29, 33, 35–39, 42, 45–46, 48–49, 74–75, 118, 129, 133, 178, 192, 223, 228

Architecture, 23, 38, 46–49, 207, 211

Armour, 64, 208

Artifact, 19, 83, 89, 139, 142, 178–179

Asynchronous, 84, 87, 223, 231

B

Baseline, 33, 108, 121, 124–128, 142, 216

Beck, 65

Beedle, 167

Bekkering, 85

Bergin, ii, 210

Biehl, 49, 142

Blame, 108, 159, 203

Bottleneck, 39

Braithwaite, 180

Brooks, 35

Budget, 9, 44, 64, 104, 116, 146

Build, 4, 7, 20, 22, 30, 34–35, 47, 52, 55, 68, 87, 90, 99–108, 111–112, 116, 142, 153, 161, 171, 182, 193, 204, 206, 208, 224

Business value, 4, 18, 23–25, 43, 46, 57, 80, 93, 95, 113–114, 116, 118, 120, 122, 124, 126, 128–130, 132, 134, 136, 138–140, 142, 145–146, 166, 208, 218, 228

C

Candidate, 42

Capability Maturity Model, 5, 197

Carmel, 12–13, 51, 57, 62, 73, 75, 77, 197, 201

Central coordination, 55

Change, iii, 3–4, 7, 16, 28, 35, 38, 57–58, 89, 93, 99, 109–110, 120, 136–139, 141, 145, 151, 153, 160–162, 165, 169, 177, 179, 184–185, 195, 197, 199, 203–204, 206, 214–218, 221, 230

Chief architect, 35–37, 42, 74–75, 129, 133, 223

Christerson, ii, 30, 41

Churchill, 204

CMMI, 5, 197–199

Coach, iii, 30, 33, 39–41, 44–45, 129–130, 133, 135, 149, 156, 188, 195, 200, 216

Cockburn, 15

Code, 37, 88, 104–112, 119, 172, 174, 176–180, 185, 196, 198, 229

Cohn, 118, 124–125, 132

Collaboration, 1–2, 8, 11, 16, 21–22, 24, 30, 32, 35, 51, 55–56, 60, 71, 82–83, 87–91, 120, 163–164, 170, 173, 177, 183, 190, 223

Collocation, 16, 28, 205

Command-and-control, 21, 66, 214

Communication, iii, 1, 4, 9, 11–12, 19–20, 23–24, 26–28, 30, 32–33, 35,

Q

R

S

9 783947 991273

10
unidades

ISBN 9798717981804

9 798717 981804